MAKE TUMBLR WORK FOR YOUR BUSINESS

The complete guide to marketing your business, generating leads, finding new customers and building your brand on Tumblr.

Alex Stearn

Copyright © 2014 Alex Stearn

All rights reserved.

ISBN-13:978-1502911339
ISBN-10:1502911337

© 2014 by Alex Stearn
Exterior cover, internal design and contents © Alex Stearn
All rights reserved.
The rights to reproduce the work are reserved to the copyright holder.

No part of this publication may be reproduced, stored in a retrieval system, distributed, or transmitted in any form or by any means, electronic or mechanical, photocopying, recording, scanning or otherwise without the prior written permission of the publisher, except in the case of brief quotations embodied in critical reviews and certain other non commercial uses permitted by copyright law. For permission requests, write to the publisher, Alex Stearn.

All the business names, product names and brand names used in this book are trademarks, trade names or registered trademarks of their respective owners and I am not associated with any product, business entity or company. The views, opinions and strategies in this book are purely those of the author.

Limit of Liability / Disclaimer of Warranty. While the publisher and author have used their best efforts in preparing this book, they make no representations or warranties with the respect to the accuracy or completeness of the contents of this book specifically disclaim any implied warranties of merchantability or fitness for a particular purpose. No warranty maybe created or extended by sales representatives or written sales materials. The advice and strategies contained herein may not be suitable for your situation. You should consult with a professional where appropriate. Neither the publisher or the author shall be liable for any loss of profit or any commercial damages, including but not limited to special, incidental, consequential, or other damages.

Although the author and publisher have made every effort to ensure that the information in this book was correct at press time, the author and publisher do not assume and hereby disclaim any liability to any party for any loss, damage, or disruption caused by errors or omissions, whether such errors or omissions result from negligence, accident, or any other cause. While every effort is made to ensure that all the information in this book is accurate and up to date, we accept no responsibility for keeping the information up to date or any liability for any failure to do so.

Copyright © 2014 Alex Stearn

All rights reserved.

ISBN-13:978-1502911339
ISBN-10:1502911337

This book is dedicated
to Sonia, Tony and Ollie.

Other Books in the Series

Make Social Media Work For Your Business

Make Facebook Work For Your Business

Make Twitter Work For Your Business

Make Instagram Work For Your Business

Make Pinterest Work For Your Business

Make Google + Work For Your Business

Make YouTube Work For Your Business

Table of Contents

Why This Book? 1

Chapter One
The Importance of Understanding Social Media Marketing
7

Chapter Two
How to Run a Successful Tumblr Marketing Campaign, an Overview 23

Chapter Three
Getting Started on Tumblr 31

Chapter Four
Content is King on Tumblr 41

Chapter Five
Building your Audience on Tumblr 57

Chapter Six
Day to Day Activity 65

Chapter Seven
Measuring and Monitoring your Results _____ 67

Chapter Eight
Building your Brand with Tumblr _____ 73

Chapter Nine
The Essential Tumblr Marketing Plan _____ 87

Chapter Ten
Preparing your Business for Success _____ 95

Chapter Eleven
The Icing on The Cake _____ 105

Why This Book?

SO YOU WANT to launch a Tumblr marketing campaign for your business or maybe you've already done so and you're just not achieving the results you expected. Perhaps that's because you've found it difficult to build a sizeable following or your audience is simply not converting into paying customers.

Every day hundreds of businesses are setting out on their social media journey excited about the opportunities and possibilities that this relatively new type of marketing may be able to offer their business. Some are getting it right, reaping huge rewards and managing to leverage the enormous power of the internet through Tumblr but the majority are struggling to make it work at all. Those who are struggling often don't really understand exactly how social media works and launch into a campaign without any plan or strategy or without even knowing exactly what they are looking to achieve. They perhaps create Tumblr, ask their web developer to add a follow button on their website, invite their friends and customers to join them and then start posting updates. After a while they realise that whatever they are doing is having little or no positive effect on their sales and they are all left with the same questions:

- How do I leverage the almighty power of the internet and Tumblr to make money for my business?

- How do I find the people who are interested in my products?

- How do I draw these people away from Tumblr and onto my website or blog?

- And the ultimate question, how do I convert all these people into paying customers and actually profit from Tumblr marketing?

These businesses either continue to go round in circles waiting for a miracle to happen, give up altogether or continue to believe that there is a way they can make social media work for their business and start looking for a solution to solve their problem.

This is exactly what I did and this is where my social media journey began. I started to look for a solution but kept coming up with the same brick walls, the same fluffy vague information about engagement and lots of very expensive courses. I read books and blogs but they never really seemed to solve my problem and get to the heart of the matter.

I then decided to make it my mission to demystify the hype surrounding social media marketing and discover everything I possibly could about how to make Tumblr and all the other major social media platforms work for any business. I studied literally hundreds of campaigns to see what was working and what wasn't and completely immersed myself in social media marketing until all my questions were answered. My aim was to discover how to utilise the power of Tumblr and all the other major social platforms to help any business achieve their marketing goals. I made it my mission to leave no stone unturned in terms of a marketing opportunity which could help any business generate leads and ultimately increase their sales.

After 18 months of immersing myself in this subject I am now delighted to hand this information over to you. My goal is to help you save your time and your resources and provide you with a highly effective system to make Tumblr work for your business. In this book I am going to share with you everything you need to know to take your business to the next level, and leverage the power of Tumblr marketing, so you can achieve the highest profits, the best customers, the best ambassadors for your business and make money 24/7.

This book is perfect for anyone who is seriously committed to growing their business and achieving incredible results. Whether you are just starting out or already up and running and uncertain how to make Tumblr work for your business then this book is to going to teach you exactly how to do just that. You will have absolutely everything you need to learn, prepare, plan and implement a campaign which is going to help you generate leads and find new customers.

The fact is, Tumblr and social media as a whole, is a game changer, a dream come true for any business and has completely revolutionised the way business is being done today. However, it is still just a marketing tool and while on the face of it seems free, if not used correctly and effectively it is simply just a waste of your time and resources.

In this book you will not only learn the skills and strategies of marketing on Tumblr but also everything you need to know about how social media works in marketing and how to plan, prepare and execute your campaign including:

- What social media marketing is, why it is so good, why it is absolutely essential for any business today and why so many businesses are getting it wrong.

- The psychology behind why people make buying decisions and how you can use this knowledge to succeed in your Tumblr campaign and on other social platforms as well.

- The importance of defining your business, your brand and your target audience and how to do this.

- How to set clear goals and objectives for your social media campaign.

- How to prepare your website or blog for success, capture leads and build a highly targeted list of subscribers.

- How to plan, create, maintain and manage your Tumblr campaign.

- Detailed information about how to set up your business profile on Tumblr.

- The strategies you need to implement to attract the best prospects and build and maintain a targeted following on Tumblr and build lasting relationships.

- The importance of content and how to easily find ideas to create content for your page.

- How to convert your followers into leads, paying customers and ambassadors and brand advocates of your business.

- How to constantly measure and monitor your campaign so you can steer your campaign to achieve your goals.

A great deal of love has gone into the writing of this book, love of the subject itself and the fact that after researching and devoting 18 months to writing this book and the other books in the series I can finally hand over this information and knowledge to you so you can benefit and profit from my findings. I hope you will be inspired and your business will thrive and flourish as a result of reading and implementing the suggested strategies.

A great deal of love has gone into the writing of this book, love of the subject itself and the fact that after researching and devoting 18 months to writing this book and the other books in the series I can finally hand over this information and knowledge to you so you can benefit and profit from my findings. I hope you will be inspired and your business will thrive and flourish as a result of reading and implementing the suggested strategies.

Even within the time it has taken to write this book, certain things have changed in the social media world and so some sections have been updated to reflect those changes. The world of social media is dynamic and therefore it is my commitment to keep updating this book as and when those changes occur. If you wish to keep up to date with latest social media updates, tips and changes please subscribe to my newsletter at www.alexstearn.com

As mentioned above there are books available for each of the major social platforms including, Facebook, Google, Twitter, LinkedIn™, SlideShare, YouTube, Pinterest and Instagram.

Chapter One

The Importance of Understanding Social Media Marketing

BEFORE LAUNCHING INTO your Tumblr marketing campaign and so that you are absolutely committed when you do start you will need to be convinced that social media marketing does actually work for business and that you are going to be able to make it work for yours. In this chapter you will learn why social media marketing has gained so much attention, why so many brands are using it and why it is so different from other forms of marketing. The aim here is to help you to truly appreciate the power and importance of this relatively new method of marketing. Once you are totally convinced that the time you will be investing will be truly worthwhile you will be ready to launch into your Tumblr marketing campaign with strength, confidence and conviction.

So what is social media exactly? Social media is the place where people connect with other people using the technology we have today. It's where people engage, share, co-operate, interact, learn, enjoy and build relationships. The number of ways in which we connect with each other has grown massively in recent years from telephone, mobiles, email, text, video, newspaper or radio to what we have today, the social media networks.

As humans the majority of us want to belong, be accepted, loved, respected and heard. We are social animals and social media has provided us with new tools that allow us to be more social even if our lives are more hectic and we are living a long way from our friends and family. It's now not unusual for family and friends to be located at opposite sides of the country or even in a different country. Our lives have become far busier and more transient than ever and yet we still crave the same social connections as we did 100 years ago when we would probably have been living in the same village or town as our family and friends.

The impact that social media is having on our lives and on businesses is massive, social media has completely changed the way we communicate and the way we do everything. It has made connecting with people and building relationships so much easier, now staying in contact with someone we may only have met once is straight forward, we can find old friends we went to school or college with and the opportunities for making new contacts is limitless. Social media has given us the ability to quickly and easily share ideas, experiences and information on anything we like and we can find out about anyone, any business or anything. With the massive growth in smart phone ownership most people can now access the internet instantly, we are living in a virtual world and we can literally connect to anyone, from anywhere, at anytime.

Understanding the reasons why people love social media so much will help give you a really good idea about how, as a business, you need to engage so you can maintain and grow your audience. Most people are on social media to be social, to connect with other family and friends and have fun. However here are a few more reasons why so many use and love social media:

To be part of a community or common interest group.
To express their feelings and have a voice.
To reconnect with old college or school friends.
To find out where their friends are.
To tell their friends where they are.
To find out if a product or service is good.
To connect with thought leaders.
To make business contacts.

To follow brands.
To keep up to date with current affairs, football scores, etc.
To connect with famous people.
To find inspiration and motivation.
To learn by reading blogs, watching videos and listening to podcasts.
To help other people.
To launch a business.
To advertise and grow a business.
To make new friends.
To make new contacts.
To connect with others in different countries.
To make a difference.
To be entertained.
To communicate quickly and save time.
To support important causes or people.
To find a job.

The power and enormity of social media
Everyone is doing Social! Ok, so not everyone is doing social media but the majority of people are! Wherever you go you will see somebody with their heads down looking at some device and you can bet your bottom dollar that they are accessing some social site whether it's Tumblr, Facebook, Twitter, Instagram, LinkedIn, YouTube, Google+, Pinterest or Snapchat.

The growth in social media is huge and it's no wonder that it is being called 'The Social Media Revolution.' Without going into too much statistical information it's safe to say that your customer is probably using at least one social network either for personal or business use and very likely to be accessing multiple sites.

All the social media platforms are growing at incredible speeds and you only have to type 'Social media statistics' into Google and you will blown away by the millions and billions. At the last count Tumblr has 184 million Blogs, Facebook now has over 1 billion users, more than 1 billion unique users visit YouTube per month and Twitter has 215 monthly active users. The most popular websites are social. The world loves Social.

What is Social Media Marketing

Not long ago promoting a business could feel very much like being alone on a desert island. You could have a great idea but unless you had vast sums of money for television, magazine or direct mail advertising then frustratingly your idea was very likely to remain a secret. Today it is totally different and social media has given businesses endless opportunities to reach their target audience, connect with new prospects and enter new markets. The playing field has been levelled out and now anyone with the right knowledge has more chance than ever of making their business a success.

Social media marketing is a relatively new form of marketing and refers to the processes, strategies and tactics used by businesses on social networking sites and blogs to gain attention and ultimately increase their revenue. Businesses and large brands are now using the fact that people love to engage and connect with other people with the other very important fact that they are very likely to find their target audience on social media so that they can do the following:

- Find, reach and connect with potential customers.

- Drive traffic to a website or blog.

- Stay connected with, and communicate with, existing customers. It is a well known fact that existing customers are far more likely to purchase and also pay more for a product than someone who has not bought before.

- To build trust, interest and loyalty by interacting with your followers (potential customers) so that ultimately they will purchase your product, continue to purchase your products and hopefully recommend your product to their friends.

- To produce content that users will share with their social network or recommend to their friends. Social media marketing strongly centres around the creation of content for a particular audience with the intention that it can be shared , liked and commented by on the user. When this happens the content is being passed to other users by word of mouth, the most powerful form of advertising.

- To listen and find out what your customers want.

The Big Link, The Psychology Behind Buying Behaviour

Not only have successful marketeers recognised that people want to engage with people, they have also tapped into the psychology behind why people make buying decisions and incorporated this into their social media campaigns.

As a business you will need to understand a great deal about your customers in order to market your products successfully to your target audience. Understanding how and why people make the final purchase decision will go a long way in understanding how you can actually make Tumblr marketing work for your business. There seem to be a number of factors that influence consumers when they are making their buying decision. Leveraging and using this knowledge with your Tumblr campaign is incredibly powerful and a recipe for success.

The Like Factor
This is a Biggie. When we look at the findings and the psychology behind buying decisions it often comes down to simply being likeable.

Consumers are far more likely buy a product from someone they like, respect or trust. Word of mouth advertising has always proven to be the most powerful form of advertising and now Tumblr has taken this to another level and managed to harness this online with the 'like' and the 'reblog' buttons. Having your business name or brand reach hundreds or even thousands of people is now possible and someone only has to 'like' or interact with your business on social media and you can almost guarantee that someone else will see it. The truth is people do business with people they like and are more likely to spread the word to their network about deals and special offers from people they like, trust and respect.

Social proof
When a consumer finds themselves at a point of indecision they will look for social proof and seek advice and corroboration from others. They are far more likely to buy if they see that their friends or a similar group of people have bought or used product. People generally look to others for advice or look to see what others are buying to get over their personal insecurity when making a buying decision. This is why you see so many women shopping in pairs, the opinion of a friend about an item can often be the deciding factor when making the decision to buy or not.

The reason this is so powerful with social media marketing is simply because seeing a large number of people 'liking' a product or service can be enough to persuade someone to make a buying decision, to read something or follow a business. The truth is that people trust the opinion of others more than they trust advertising and in order to make social media marketing work then businesses need to leverage this fact.

Authority and reviews
Even before the internet was introduced people have been keen to find reviews about products they were interested in buying particularly if they were planning to make a major purchase. They would either buy a special magazine or seek information from an authoritative figure on a TV

advertisement. Today however shoppers are far more savvy, they can smell an advert a mile off and they will go out of their way to find honest reviews about something they may want to buy. They are also spoilt for choice not only with the number of products available to them but they can find a review about literally anything just by a simple search on the internet or looking at a brand's social media page. People always have and always will want as much evidence as possible that they are making the right buying decision. Any business who wants to succeed today needs to embrace this fact and try and gain as many reviews for their products and services as possible. Reviews could be in the form of customer blog articles, reviews on your website, on social media sites or articles in newspapers and magazines. Displaying articles, client testimonials or the logos of magazines that you have been featured in on your website will also go a long way to building authority and gaining the trust of your prospects.

Scarcity or exclusivity

Scarcity or exclusivity can play a big part in people buying decisions and Tumblr can be a perfect place to communicate and use this factor to sell your products. If a product is scarce or less available the consumer will often perceive that this product has greater value and as they become less available the consumer fears that they may lose out on a great deal or a one time offer. Giving your prospects a deadline or a specific time to purchase something or redeem an offer is an incredibly powerful way of focussing their mind to make a decision. When they know they need to make that decision by a certain time or they may lose out on a one time deal they are far more likely to make that decision. Another very effective way of using this factor is by simply suggesting to your prospects that by signing up for your email opt-in, they will be the first to hear about your new products, or your exclusive offers.

Consistency

Consumers do not like taking risks and often prefer to repeat their past purchasing behaviour by buying from a brand they have bought from before. The majority of shoppers are brand loyal and social media is another way of nurturing this type of behaviour by building up even deeper relationships with your customers through constant contact and updates.

Reciprocation

Reciprocation is a very powerful factor to take into consideration if you are looking to succeed on Tumblr. As humans, the majority of us have a natural desire to repay favours and with Tumblr you can really put this into practise. If you show support by either liking, Relogging or commenting on other peoples content not only will it attract their attention they will, more often than not, return the favour by 'liking,' commenting and reblogging your content. Also if you are sharing great content on your network or offering good, valuable and free advice you are very likely to earn a great deal of respect and this will often result in a good pay back of some sort.

Why is Social Media Marketing So Good for your Business?

We know that an enormous number of people are accessing the social networks to connect with each other and now we need to understand why this type of marketing is so different from other forms of marketing and why it is so important for your business. The main reason is that social media marketing is fundamentally more effective. Consumers today are smart, they are tired and suspicious of traditional forms of advertising, more often than not they will fast forward a TV commercial, switch channel or skip a printed page with an advertisement on it. Todays consumers want to hear that a product has been tried and tested, they want to see a product being demonstrated and they often need a recommendation from a trusted source to make a purchase, most probably a friend. Here are some reasons why social media marketing is more effective than other more traditional marketing methods:

Social media offers you the opportunity to find the right target audience
Never before has it been so easy to find and access your target audience. With the information that Tumblr and most of the social networks hold about their users you can now target and find the very people who are more likely to buy your products or services.

Social media allows you to have a direct contact with your customer
Literally you have the opportunity to communicate directly and stay in touch with your customer, unlike traditional forms of advertising.

Social media marketing harnesses the power of peer recommendation
A recent online study showed that 78% of people trust recommendations by others. Social media marketing is the only media that can harness the most powerful form of advertising, word of mouth, by making it possible for consumers to communicate with each other and vote for products or services by pressing the 'like' or 'follow' button.

Helps builds your brand
Never has there been so much opportunity to build your brand. Your brand is simply the most valuable asset of your business. Your brand is what differentiates you from other businesses, it is the image people have of your business and it establishes loyalty. With social media you have the opportunity to engage with consumers and build positive brand associations in a way that no other media can. Consumers now have the choice and opportunity to follow your brand and if they do, this means they actually want to hear or see what you have to say.

Humanises your brand
Social media allows you to communicate with your audience in a totally unique way. Your brand is no longer a rigid logo but a personality, not only can you show your appreciation and the value you place on your audience but they can also grow to love your brand too. No other type of

marketing allows this type of two way live communication.

Offers continual exposure to your product
Social media marketing allows you to be continually in contact with your followers. Once you have your audience they can hear from you and see your brand on a daily basis. Statistics prove that on average a person needs to see or connect with a brand 7 times before they buying it. This is a difficult and costly goal to achieve with traditional forms of advertising but incredibly easy with social media marketing.

The Consumer has a choice
Unlike other traditional methods of advertising the consumer has the opportunity to be exposed to your product by choice, they can opt in or out whenever they want.

Your audience is relaxed and receptive
The majority of people are accessing social accounts to be social and in their own leisure time. Social media is all about connecting with friends and relatives, meeting new people and making new contacts. People are far more receptive to hearing from a brand in their own time when they are relaxed, as long as the brand is not continually pushing their product.

You can continually engage with your audience
Social media marketing allows you to have an ongoing dialogue with your audience like no other media. Fans or followers who have interacted with a business on social media are far more likely to visit their online store than those who did not.

It's viral
Once your followers choose to interact or share your content then this interaction is seen by their network of friends who are then also exposed to your brand. This is how viral growth happens which results in audience growth and brand awareness, more prospects, more customers and increased sales.

Social media is an asset to your business
Unlike other forms of advertising where you see your marketing investment disappear your Tumblr or any other social account becomes a valuable asset. If you are using your social media marketing correctly your network will grow, you will be building trust and your asset will increase in value. With traditional advertising once an advert is delivered the connection with the buyer is over and you see your investment literally disappear.

It is like having your own broadcasting channel
Once you have your campaign set up and your follower numbers are growing, you literally have your very own broadcasting channel which you own. You can communicate with your followers about anything 24/7. Nobody can take this away unless of course you are not running it correctly and you are losing followers. If you provide content that is so useful and interesting, your followers will keep coming back again and again to check if you have anything new to say. You then have a following of people who will associate your valuable content and their positive experience with your brand.

You can offer your customers proof of trading
Having a social media presence which is active and engaging helps to reassure customers that your business actually exists. They can easily check, by comments left by customers, whether your business is reputable and trustworthy and they are far more likely to buy from you once they see your active presence on social media.

Improve your search engine ranking
Google counts social sharing when ranking your website or blog. If people are finding your content valuable then the search engines will register that and then rank you accordingly. Social media sites are highly ranked in the search engines and having a well optimised profile is yet another way of being found on the internet.

Opens up a worldwide playing field
It used to be only the large companies who could afford to build their brand and have the opportunity to access thousands of potential customers. Now everybody with a business has the opportunity to reach thousands of people both nationally and globally, grow their business and benefit from one of the most powerful forms of marketing. Having a business no longer has to be a lonely island you literally have the opportunity to get your message heard by thousands of people through social networking.

Provides advantages for the consumer
With just a few clicks of the mouse or the tap of a smart phone, consumers can be in contact with any business very quickly. For once their opinions are important, taken seriously and valued, they can contact a brand for customer service issues or just follow a brand because they are interested. For the first time they have a voice and a very powerful one. This is showing in the continual rise in the number of people following brands. People want to remain close to the brands they are interested in.

You can listen to your customers
You can now hear what your customers are saying about your product or service and you can use this information to improve or develop your products and improve your customer service. This will result in your business becoming more transparent and shows your customers that you care and value their opinion which ultimately leads to more trust for your brand.

You can become a thought leader
By producing valuable and rich content for your audience you can become a thought leader. Not only will this help if you are a personal brand but will also help in building respect and reputation for any business or brand.

You can make a difference
With social media you can actually make a positive difference to people's lives. Once you know your audience you can provide content for them which is of value to them and is actually going to help them in some way. Helping your audience like this goes a long way and will hopefully result in them remembering your business when they are ready to make that purchasing decision.

Endless opportunities
Never has there been so much opportunity to have direct access to so many people and neither has there been so much opportunity for businesses of any size to have ongoing contact with so many of their potential customers. This is a marketeer or business owner's dream.

IS SOCIAL MEDIA ACTUALLY WORKING FOR BUSINESS?

It is evident that the majority of major brands are running successful social media marketing campaigns. These brands are investing huge amounts of money, time and resources into this type of marketing, however you don't have to go too far to see whether social media marketing is actually working for business, simply ask yourself these questions:

- Would you prefer to buy a product if you knew that a friend or somebody you know of had tried it?

- Would you prefer to buy a product from a business or person that you do know rather than a business or person that you don't know?

- If you were thinking of buying a product from a business you had no history with, would you go and look to see if they had a social media site and see what other people were saying about their product?

If you answered yes to these questions then you can be pretty sure that social media marketing does actually work for businesses. It has to work doesn't it?

Why So Many Businesses are Getting it Wrong

Even though most business owners have heard how powerful social media marketing can be the majority are still unsure as to how to use it to benefit their business. So many Tumblr's have been created with enthusiasm only to be abandoned a couple of months even weeks down the line. Others are painstakingly posting consistently every day but posting the wrong type of content without a clue how to get their followers to buy their products. Many businesses are just paying lip service and seem to think that displaying a few social media icons on their site is enough to miraculously increase their revenue and some are not even connected to any networks at all. Although on the face of it, social media marketing seems free it actually takes a sizeable investment of man hours, and if you are getting it wrong you may as well be throwing a great deal of money out of the window. Here are some common reasons why so many businesses are getting it wrong:

Not 100% committed and convinced

Many businesses are not convinced that it actually works at all and therefore are not prepared to put in the time it takes to learn how to plan and implement the effective strategies it takes to build a successful campaign. As a result their campaign falls flat and they simply give up after a few months.

Little or no understanding about how social media marketing works

Many still think that setting up a profile and putting an icon on their website is what it's all about. They may even post a few status updates and post some pictures of their product in the hope that their website is suddenly going to be inundated with new traffic and think that these new visitors are miraculously going to convert into customers.

They don't understand the fact that followers are worthless unless they know what to do with them

Just because a business has maybe 1000 or 30,000 followers or followers, does not mean this will automatically transfer to their balance sheet. Followers are just followers, and as long a business doesn't know what do with those followers they will stay as just followers and not customers.

Not understanding the psychology behind buying decisions

They have absolutely no idea about the psychology behind how and why people make buying decisions and therefore, do not know how to use this knowledge to their advantage in their campaign.

Lack of clear goals

Aimlessly sharing content on their network without setting specific and measurable goals is just a waste of time and resources.

Not having a system to capture and convert leads

Building a following is almost useless if those followers are not visiting the business' website or subscribing to the newsletter so that they can be converted into paying customers. Many businesses are still not making lead capture one of their main goals.

Unrealistic expectations

Social media is a long terms strategy, it needs to be an integral part of a business' marketing plan and today it's as important as any other daily task a business may undertake. It is not a one size fits all solution and is not a solution for overnight success. It takes careful planning and long term commitment.

The wrong audience

It's no good having a huge number of followers if they are not the correct audience. There are even sites where you can buy followers, but if they are not the right audience then they are very unlikely to be interested in what that business has to offer.

Not enough followers
The majority of businesses are going to need a sizeable audience to make any impact at all, and although engagement is important, unless a business has a healthy number of followers it's not going to be a great deal of benefit.

Not being proactive
Many businesses seem to assume that people are just going to press the 'like' or 'follow' button on their blog or website. Unfortunately it doesn't work like that and people generally need a good reason or incentive to follow a business, unless it's a very well known brand.

Trying to push their products all the time
This is not what social media marketing is about and businesses that continually push their products are just missing the whole point of how social media marketing works and will lose followers as a result.

Posting too little, posting too often, or posting the wrong content altogether
If you post too much your posts will be considered as spam. If you post too little you will just be forgotten and if you post the wrong content you will not attract the right audience which may harm your brand. In an online survey top three reasons for losing followers were:
i.) The Company posted too frequently
ii.) The business pushed their products too much
iii.) The business posted offensive content

Chapter Two

How to Run a Successful Tumblr Marketing Campaign, an Overview

ONCE YOU HAVE made the decision to be 100% committed to your campaign, you fully understand the theory behind it and you plan and implement the strategies and tactics outlined in this book your business is going to reap the benefits and you will in time develop an extremely valuable asset. One thing is for certain if you choose to ignore social media you can be sure that your competition will not and you'll be allowing them to steal the advantage. Social media is a powerful way to increase your revenue by driving sales, increasing customer loyalty and building your brand while at the same time pushing down your cost of sales, marketing, customer service and much more. Now let's get started!

So how do you leverage the power of social media and put it to work to benefit your business and produce amazing results? This chapter is designed to give you a brief overview about what is required to build a successful campaign so that as and when you read each chapter it will make more sense. Every aspect of this overview and everything you need to do and implement will be mapped out clearly for you in the subsequent chapters.

The opportunity to reach an unlimited number of new contacts and prospects is available to every business today. You can safely say that your prospects are out there and all you need to do is know where to find them, how to connect with them and then how to capture and convert them into your customers.

Successful businesses are using Tumblr and the other social media platforms in a totally different way to that of traditional methods of marketing. With marketing on Tumblr there is no need to employ pushy sales techniques. Once you put the essential work, planning and system in place you will find your products are practically selling themselves and your prospects are buying your products and becoming your brand advocates as a natural progression from your initial contact with them. The whole process is straight forward and as long as you carry out the necessary background work, planning and preparation you can make it work for your business.

Know what you want
You need to have a very good idea where you want your business to be in the next 1–3 years, if you don't know what you want then it is unlikely that your business will achieve anywhere near its potential. When you have a clear vision for your business it helps you to focus and create the necessary goals you need to put into place to achieve that vision.

Define your business and your brand and your target audience
Brands establish customer loyalty and Tumblr offers you a huge opportunity to build your brand. In order to communicate in the right way you need to create and consistently deliver the right message and brand experience to your prospects and customers. To do this you need to define your business and define and understand your target audience so you can create your brand.

Plan, plan, plan
Social media is not a quick fix, the majority of businesses start a campaign and then fall by the wayside. If you want to grow your business then careful planning is required which involves: creating your mission statement, setting clear and measurable goals and objectives, planning your system for lead capture and planning your content strategy in line with who and what your target audience want. Putting a good

plan and system into place will take all the guess work, worry and stress out of your campaign and give you confidence and direction. You will find that the campaign will be almost running itself and working like a machine producing leads and customers. Without a carefully crafted plan your campaign is extremely unlikely to succeed and you will waste huge amounts of time and resources.

Prepare your business
Before launching your campaign you need to prepare your whole business so your brand and your brand message is evident throughout. You will need to communicate your brand through everything your do or say including all your marketing material, brochures, promotional material, your website, your blog and your email.

Your website is one of the best sales people you can have, it works 24/7 and can turn up in your customer's home at the click of a mouse. When your prospect arrives on your website you need to make them feel they have arrived at the right place and that you understand their needs and can either provide a solution or give them exactly what they want. If you already have a website then you need to check it has all the necessary features it takes to grab your visitors attention, deliver the right message, capture them and convert them into customers. Statistics prove that unless a business has a clever method of capturing leads then the majority of visitors to a website will leave without buying anything or ever returning again. Therefore before even starting your Tumblr campaign you will need to check or create your website so that it does the job it is supposed to which is to capture leads and convert them into customers.

Set up your email campaign
Email is still one of the most effective methods of converting leads and therefore you will need to set up an account with an email service provider and plan your email campaign so you can continue to build a relationship with your prospect, build trust and sell your products.

Create your Tumblr

Your Tumblr will in many cases be the first impression your prospects have about your business and is as important as your website or blog. The aim of your Tumblr is to capture your prospects so that you can continue to communicate and build a relationship with them through their newsfeed and through email. It is unlikely that the majority of your followers will return to your blog after their initial visit so your blog needs to grab their attention and make your prospects take action as soon as they arrive by liking your page and joining your opt-in list.

Create your Tumblr posting calendar

Social media is not like traditional forms of advertising so frequently pushing your products, posting adverts and plugging your business is not going to work and is likely to lose you followers. One of the most important things you are going to have to do for a successful Tumblr campaign is to regularly produce and post compelling content that your audience actually wants to engage with and share. Tumblr marketing is all about selling without selling and the aim of producing content is not to directly sell your products but to do the following:

- Boost traffic to your website, generate, capture and nurture leads
- Create brand awareness
- Constantly remind your audience of your brand so when they are ready to buy they buy from you
- Improve your ranking in the search engines
- Create engagement, build relationships and encourage your audience to share your content with their friends
- Support others by liking, commenting on and sharing their content
- Stand out as a thought leader and build your reputation as an expert in your industry
- Create such good content that your audience stays liking your page and continuing to read your updates which builds and

encourage brand loyalty

Your content is where you can connect with your audience through their interests and passions. Your quality of content needs to be outstanding and you need to delight your audience with the best possible fresh, new and compelling material, excellence is what you should be aiming for every time you post. The biggest thing to remember is that you need to tailor all your content to your audience's desires and needs.

Once you are absolutely clear about who your target audience is, what makes them tick, and what their values and aspirations are you can determine what subjects and topics they will be interested in. The majority of the content you post will need to be about their needs and not yours. There is nothing more off putting and likely to lose you followers than continually posting about your business and shouting about your products or services. Of course you can do this occasionally if you have new products or special offers but you need to be selective otherwise your posts just become bad noise. Remember your followers are mostly on Tumblr to be inspires and to be social and if your posts ruin this experience they will associate your brand with a bad experience and it won't be long before you start losing your followers and potential customers.

When you have decided on the subjects and topics you are going to create content about, then you will need to create a Tumblr posting calendar which will help you to consistently deliver this high quality content. You will need to incorporate everything in this calendar including any events you are planning, any special industry events, public holidays, blog posts, videos and offers or contests you may be planning. You then need to map it all out so you know exactly how you are going to promote them on Tumblr with the functionality you have available to do so.

Build a sizeable and highly targeted following

The main aim of building your audience is to grow a community of followers who are interested in your products, will engage with your content and become advocates for your brand. In order to have any impact at all you are going to need a sizeable number of targeted followers on Tumblr. Building your audience is going to be an ongoing task and involve many different strategies all covered in this book. The size and time it takes to build your audience will depend on the time and resources you have available. However, do not get overwhelmed about building an audience of thousands of followers, it's more important to concentrate your efforts on targeting the right audience and then delighting them with great content. This way you will benefit from everything that goes with a highly engaged audience by delivering a great brand experience and you will find your audience naturally growing in a very positive way.

The essential day to day activity

To build a strong presence, build trust, build relationships and reputation you will need to be active and nurture your followers. Social media is not a one way street, it's an ongoing two way communication, it's about going out and showing that you are interested in what others have to say and it's about building community and getting your brand out there in the most positive light possible. Here are some of the things you will need to do on a day to day basis:

- Consistently post high quality content

- Follow your followers

- Engage, comment, reblog and reply to comments

- Show your audience you value and respect them

- Follow influencers in your niche

- Deal with negative comments

Analysing and measuring your campaign results

This book is all about how to make Tumblr work for your business and the only way you are going to find out if it is working or not is by constantly monitoring and analysing your results. You will need to constantly check your results against the goals and objectives you have set. Once you know what is working and what is not then you can adjust and steer your campaign accordingly, to achieve more positive results.

Chapter Three

Getting Started on Tumblr

FOUNDED IN 2007 Tumblr is a microblogging platform and social networking site which was was sold to Yahoo in 2013 for approximately 1.1 billion. Tumblr got its name from the tumblelogs which were around at the time of its creation which tended to be shorter blogs accompanied by mixed media.

Tumblr offers an amazing platform for any business or brand to promote themselves within the Tumblr's huge and active community. Every user has a dashboard where they can view the posts from the blogs they follow and can interact by liking, commenting and reblogging. Tumblr also gives brands the freedom and flexibility to customize their own blogs in line with their branding and post their own content from their dashboard including: text, images, quotes, audio, video and links. Tumblr is different from other blogs in that it is more than acceptable to produce shorter blog posts and visual only posts but also absolutely fine to post longer blog posts as well.

Tumblr has millions of unique visitors per month and there are over 100 million active blogs. With regard to the audience it has a predominantly younger user base, statistics vary but it's safe to say that approximately half of its users are under 35 and about 30% are between 35 and 49. Gender wise Tumblr has a fairly equal split between women and men and the majority of its users reside in the USA with the remaining split between the UK, Canada , Brazil and Russia. The types drawn to Tumblr seem to be predominantly in the creative, artistic or fashion industries. If this is your target then it is probably a very good idea to have an active presence on Tumblr.

BENEFITS OF TUMBLR FOR BUSINESS

Tumblr has some seriously impressive features, however before you decide to build your presence on Tumblr you need to establish whether or not you will be able to find your target audience on Tumblr. If you are targeting a younger audience then this is a very good place to start. You can do this by using the search feature, simply create an account by signing up with your email, password and username and start searching. You can either search for keywords or go to www.Tumblr.com/explore or view some popular categories and selected blogs on www.tumble.com/spotlight . You can choose to follow individual blogs or a tag where you will see all the content relating to that tag. It may also be a good idea to establish whether your competition are on Tumblr and what sort of response they are getting which you can determine by the number of notes at the bottom of their posts.

Once you have established your audience are on Tumblr and you still can't decide whether this is the right platform to promote your business, then here is some more information to help you make that decision. Tumblr has some seriously impressive features and if you are thinking of using Tumblr as another way of building your brand and promoting your products then here is a run down of the main advantages it could offer your business:

It's Free You can have a presence on a site with its own source of traffic and all for free. If you are just starting out on your blogging journey, then what better way to showcase your content, create stories, start conversations and test the market? If you are just starting out in business then you can create your permanent website for free on Tumblr which can offer you the best of both worlds, you can create a few static pages with information about your business and then also offer your followers dynamic content by posting your announcements, news and blog posts as well. Tumblr gives you all the tools to help you build your brand, create a lifestyle and tell the story about your brand and all for free. On Tumblr the possibilities are endless.

A new source of traffic If you are starting out in business then Tumblr can offer you the perfect platform with its built-in community of users. With literally millions of users Tumblr will offer you traffic that you would never have had without having a presence on the platform.

User friendly It is incredibly straightforward to set up a blog and you need absolutely no technical knowledge to do so, which means it's quick and easy to get going.

A new source of traffic Tumblr has its own community, therefore its own source of traffic. With literally millions of users on Tumblr your blog has more of a chance of being viewed by the community of users which already exists on the platform. Users can simply search for blogs they are interested in from their home page.

It's visual Tumblr is very visual in nature and therefore businesses that are creative tend to benefit the most, for example; photography, graphic design, fashion and jewellery design. However there are many categories that are still very successful on Tumblr and you only have to look on Tumblr's spotlight page to view the diversity of businesses and interests.

You can find new customers on Tumblr Tumblr like other social networks gives you the opportunity to find your customers and interact and engage with your audience. You can like and reblog posts (share posts) and likewise people can like or reblog your posts. Tumblr is renowned for a very engaged and active community of people who like to share. Tumblr does not support comments but if you want to add the function you can do so by adding either Disqus or Facebook comments. Facebook comments can be a little more complex to install but can offer you the best of both worlds and increase traffic to your blog from Facebook.

Very passionate users Tumblr is home to some of the most engaged communities and users are not only passionate about their niche but also about Tumblr and are completely hooked on the platform. It is therefore an excellent platform to become involved in and if you produce good content other users are very likely to either like or reblog.

Flexible The great thing about Tumblr is it is incredibly versatile, it's perfectly acceptable to produce long or short blog posts and posts can be just a few sentences long if you like. If you do not consider yourself a writer and writing long blog posts is not one of your strength then Tumblr is an ideal platform.

You can customise your blog You can customise your blog by using any of the free or premium designs and which is ideal if you want to keep your Tumblr in line with your branding.

You have full control You have absolute control of your site or blog on Tumblr. There are no character limitations, no file limitations and no advertising next to your content. You have full control to tell your story with whatever media you choose whether it's image, text, links, chat, video or audio. In addition the mobile app offers you the functionality to post anything from anywhere.

Choose your own domain You can choose a custom domain and therefore have a domain that will easily be remembered and associated with your brand.

Another way to get found through organic search Tumblr is available to anyone on the web, you do not have to have an account on Tumblr to view a blog on Tumblr and content is indexed by the search engines which makes it more likely to get your content found. Therefore you can use Tumblr and any of the available themes to build your own website if you like.

Long shelf life Online studies have shown that Tumblr posts have a long shelf life and things are still being reblogged long after they have been posted. In fact over one-third of reblogs on Tumblr are still occurring thirty days after the original post. This is a big advantage over some of the other platforms where posts are extremely time sensitive.

Works well with Instagram Instagram makes it very easy to share your images with Tumblr and because content on Tumblr is predominantly visual as well this is a great way of delivering similar content to two different audiences.

Use Tumblr for a particular campaign Tumblr is incredibly versatile. Many brands are using Tumblr to promote particular campaigns and then when that particular campaign is finished they can re-skin their Tumblr and use it to promote yet another campaign with a built in audience.

Backlinks Backlinks are incoming links to a website or blog coming from other sites. When people reblog your content on Tumblr then valuable backlinks are created which will help with your search engine optimisation.

A central hub Businesses often use Tumblr as a central hub for social media activity. Each piece of content has its own URL and therefore you can post all your content to all your social media platforms. You can automatically post your content to Facebook and Twitter if you wish and you can post from Instagram, YouTube, Flickr and Vimeo.

A source of talented and creative people If you are looking for incredibly talented people to create content for you then you are going to find them on Tumblr with their ready made portfolios.

A source of information Tumblr offers a huge source of information which can curate and share with your own audience if you wish. You can be really successful on Tumblr by reblogging and using other users' content without ever having to create your own. As long as you know what your target audience are interested in, you are sure to find the kind of information and visual experience they are looking for on Tumblr.

Set up multiple blogs You can set up as many blogs as you want under one username which means you can post content to different audiences without having to login and out of different accounts.

In conclusion with Tumblr you really do get the best of both worlds, the opportunity to create your own website or blog for free which is visible on the web like any other website and also the opportunity to interact and engage with an enormous community of passionate, creative and active bloggers. It's hard to turn down a free opportunity like this.

SETTING UP YOUR TUMBLR

Once you have established that your audience are on Tumblr you will need to work out what exactly you want to achieve by using Tumblr and then work out and define exactly what your goals and objectives are.

Here are some possible goals you may want to achieve through using Tumblr:
- To use Tumblr as a blog
- To use Tumblr for a particular campaign you are planning
- To use Tumblr as your main website
- To find new customers
- To build and maintain relationships with current customers
- To generate leads by building an opt-in list
- To promote your products
- To increase sales
- To build your brand

Setting up your account
Setting up your account is very straight forward and all you need to do is

sign up with an email and password and then create a username. When creating your username try and create one which is as close as possible to your business or brand name and it's also a good idea to keep your brand consistent by using the same profile picture as you do on other platforms like Facebook and Twitter.

Your description is really important since this is how you will get found by the Tumblr community and also in web search. Make sure you include industry keywords while at the same time keeping it interesting for the reader.

Tumblr really does give you the opportunity to create something quite amazing to promote and build your brand. You can add your own custom theme or choose from numerous free or premium themes which can be installed within seconds, this is extremely effective for promoting your individual style or brand. You can literally make your Tumblr an extension of your brand and you have absolute freedom when it comes to the design of your blog, if you know HTML then you can even build your own custom theme.

When it comes to the design of your blog you need to think about a number of things, not only do you need to be consistent with your brand you need to somehow communicate clearly what it is exactly that you are offering. It maybe that a follower only visits your blog once and then receives your updates in their dashboard and never comes back again. You need to hit them with what you are offering early on so when they do see your updates in their dashboard they remember each time who you are and what you offer. There are many beautiful blogs out there but often it is not obvious what they actually offer in a business sense.

As well as letting you customise your Tumblr you can also have your own domain name. Having your own custom domain not only looks more professional but also lets you take your domain with you if you do decide at a later date to change your blogging platform. To set up a custom domain simply purchase the name, for a two level domain, for example: website.com and then access your domain management centre and point the A record (ip address) to 66.6.44.4 or for three or more level domains, for example, blog.website.com, the CNAME record must point to domains.tumblr.com. This is really straightforward but if you are unclear about this simply call your domain provider's helpline, most providers are very helpful and will take you through the process with them.

Once you have done this you will need to go to your Tumblr account and click on the gear icon (Settings) and then click the pencil to the right of your 'username' section and enable 'Use a custom domain', enter your domain name and then click ' Test domain' and then 'Save.' Your domain may take up to 72 hours to take effect, up until then when you visit your domain or subdomain you will see a Tumblr error page. For more information you can visit this page http://www.tumblr.com/docs/en/custom_domains

Add comments to your blog
Tumblr does not support its own comments but having a comment system is really important if you wish to interact with your audience and start building relationships. To add comments to your blog then you can easily install Disqus comments. Simply sign up to Disqus.com and then follow the simple instructions to install which is a quick and simple procedure.

You can also add Facebook comments to Tumblr but this is a slightly more involved process and involves signing up as a Facebook developer, creating an app and adding code to your theme. Any programmer or website developer would find this straightforward or you can find numerous tutorials on the web if you want to try it yourself.

Ask me anything
This functionality offers you another way to interact with your audience and get feedback. When you have this function enabled users can ask you

anything and you can choose whether you want to publish your answers publicly or answer that question privately.

Add pages to your Tumblr

Tumblr offers you the ability to add static pages to your blog. This is particularly good if you are going to use Tumblr as your main website. You can add text, links and links with anchor text and images.

To add pages simply go to your dashboard, click on the blog you would like to edit and then on 'Customize' and then scroll to the bottom of the 'Theme' section and click on '+Add a page'

You need to add your URL after the slash /. For example, your about page could be /about. Then add a title in the 'Page title' field and then click the toggle 'Show a link to this page' and then 'Save'

To create a page with a custom layout simply select the blog you want to add it to, click on 'Customize', then click on 'Add a page' and then select 'Custom Layout' from the drop down menu on the top left. Insert your custom code into the HTML editor, then add your URL after the slash /. For example, your about page could be /about. Then click the toggle 'Show a link to this page' and 'Save'

To delete or edit a page simply find the page you would like to delete or edit and click either edit or the X icon next to the page you wish to delete.

Redirecting pages

You can redirect pages to any URL outside Tumblr if you wish. You may want to redirect a page to your website, online store or an external blog. To do this simply select the blog and then click 'Customize' and then Click on '+ Add a page.' Next select 'Redirect' from the dropdown menu on the top left and type a page URL after the slash /. For example, website or online shop. Then enter the domain URL you want to redirect to and then click the toggle 'Show a link to this page' and 'Save.'

You can also redirect pages to your posts with a specific tag. To do this simply select the blog and then click 'Customize' and then click on '+ Add a Page.' Next select 'Redirect' from the dropdown menu on the top left. Add the page ULR after the slash /, for example, www.mysite.com/mytag (the tag you want to add) and then in the 'Redirect to' field add /tagged/mytag to the end of your blog URL and replace the 'mytag' with the tag you want to use.

Add your Email opt-in

You can easily add your email sign up button to your Tumblr blog. Simply retrieve your HTML code from your email provider and then paste it into your Tumblr theme. To do this click 'Customize' and then 'Edit HTML' and then paste the code after the body tag and click the 'Update Preview' button on the top right. If you are at all unclear about this or you want it even more customised then ask your web developer to do this for you.

Notes

There are two ways you can show your appreciation on Tumblr. The first is with a like which is represented by a heart icon and the second is a reblog on Tumblr which is represented by an icon with two arrows. Likes and reblogs are collectively called notes and are displayed under your post.

Download the mobile app

Tumblr makes sharing really easy from your mobile and you can share photos, animated Gifs, video, quotes, chat, links and text and engage with your audience from anywhere. The app can be downloaded for android, iOS and Windows.

Chapter Four

Content is King on Tumblr

'THE CONTENT THAT does best is the content that surprises you.'
David Karp. Founder, Tumblr.

Because there are no follower numbers displayed on Tumblr it really is all about the content. People are following others for the quality of their content and not just because they have a large follower count.

Reblogging is incredibly powerful on Tumblr and with Tumblr your biggest aim is to have your content reblogged, when this happens your content gets shared with the followers of the person who reblogged your post and their followers followers if they are reblogged and so on. About 90% of posts on Tumblr are reblogs which illustrates that there are a huge number of users who are looking for compelling content to pass on to their followers. In turn this means that there is huge potential to get your content out there on Tumblr and start building your brand. The big advantage about Tumblr is that people are actually going out of their way to find content and reblog that content so it can be associated with their brand.

To be successful on Tumblr you really need to focus on a particular niche and find or create content for one or two topics that not only relate to your brand but also that your audience will be keen to share with their audiences. The aim is that once you find your target audience and start posting or reblogging your valuable content you will reach even more of your target audience with your carefully crafted content.

As with all social media this is not just about plugging your product it is about helping others by producing useful and relevant content which is going to be of value to them by either inspiring them or solving a problem they have.

Tumblr Posting Formats

When it comes to posting content, Tumblr is one of the most flexible platforms and provides formats for you to post text, photos, quotes, links, chat, audio and video. You can add images and text to most types of post. Here are some ideas for the type of media you can post:

Images

Tumblr is very much a picture based blogging platform and images and animated GIFs are the most popular posts counting for over 80% of content. Tumblr is a great place to tell the story of your brand with images and in order to succeed in this platform you either need to get creative by uploading your own images or spend time curating so you can reblog other users' images.

If you are a photographer or you work in a creative industry then you are most likely to have all the images or resources you need to create whatever you want for your Tumblr. However, if not, you can easily either take your own photos or source images from sites like Flickr as long as you make sure you check the terms of use. There are also many apps and sites where you can add text and graphics to your images like www.picmonkey.com or www.canva.com . There are also numerous websites where you can create images for quotes and memes.

Animated GIF's

Tumblr is where the GIF action is taking place and GIFs have made a huge contribution to its popularity, the GIF tag is one of the most popular tags on Tumblr. An animated GIF (Graphics interchange format) is a graphic image that moves, it is made up of a series of images that are displayed in succession and then loop back to the beginning when the last frame has been displayed. Because GIFs are more immediate than a video and do not require you to press the play button, a GIF offers an instant experience for the viewer which makes them an incredibly effective media for quickly communicating a message.

GIF's have huge viral potential on Tumblr and can be used for all manner of things including humour, art and also they are very good way of showing how to do something quickly. Creating an animated GIF for a video can be a very effective way of promoting and getting that video found and viewed on Tumblr. Simply create your GIF and then tag it under GIF and post it with the URL to your full length video.

With the technology available on the web creating GIFs is no longer limited to those with expert graphic design skills and creating a GIF is actually very straightforward. There are numerous tutorials on how create to do this on this page, http://brands.tumblr.com/howtogif and there are also numerous free GIF generators available like www.imgflip.com/gifgenerator that also offer a pro version.

Quotes
If you want to win with quotes then you need to know your target audience and what their needs, desires and frustrations are. Equipped with this information you can either create or reblog quotes which either inspire, motivate or help make their day better in some way.

Tumblr lets you post quotes as text only but posting a quote over an image is often more effective and is more likely to get reblogged than text only. If you are not a whizz on Photoshop then you can use sites like www.picmonkey.com which let you add text to images, crop images, add effects and add frames. Other sites like www.imgflip.com create memes.

Text
If you are concentrating on using Tumblr for longer blog posts then it's a good idea to use a theme which is designed for this type of blog, you can

find a number of designs in the 'Write a long thing' section at www.tumblr.com/themes . If you are reblogging long text posts and you want to avoid having your post truncated then simply click the reblog button and then the icon next to the gear icon and click on 'Text' which will format it for this type of post.

Audio
Tumblr lets you post audio and allows your followers to listen to music straight from your blog, it's also the perfect platform for podcasting. Tumblr offers you three different options to find the audio you want to upload in your post. You can find and upload songs with Spotify and Soundcloud who Tumblr have partnered with, or you can post the URL to a song or upload an MP3 file. Once posted a small black or white box will appear with a play and pause button.

Video
You can upload your video from your desktop or laptop or you can embed the code from a YouTube or Vimeo video. If you have your own YouTube channel then this is great way to reach a new audience and widen your reach. Even if you do not have your own contact you can still share other people's video as long as it is the sort of material that will appeal to your target audience. A short introductory video can go a long way to making that personal connection with your audience and putting a face behind your blog. Using Instagram with Tumblr can be very effective especially with Instagram's 15 second video function which is great for a quick introduction or how to video.

Chat
The purpose of the chat post is to copy and repost a chat you have had online or to re-tell a funny or interesting story. You can simply title your chat and then write the text from different characters and Tumblr will format it by separating the text and adding bold to the titles of the characters in the chat.

Link

Tumblr has its own category for link and automatically puts HTML when you add your title and URL. Once posted and a user clicks on your title in the post it will direct them straight to the URL.

IDEAS FOR CREATING CONTENT ON TUMBLR

You may be wondering how you are going to consistently produce and deliver a stream of compelling content to your audience on a regular basis for the foreseeable future. However once you have picked your topic of interest you will be surprised how one idea will lead to another and you will be able to produce a great variety of content.

Unless you are an artist or a fashion brand it is unlikely that your followers are going to want to see a constant stream of product pictures, this would be incredibly boring and will not help you to promote your brand or get the following you need for success on this platform. In order to build a real connection with your followers you will need to think of ideas for content which will appeal to your audience emotionally and get them to make friends with your brand. Your goal here needs to be to inspire and interest your followers, let them have fun and above all make them smile. Your audience want to see the personality of your business and your human side. Even businesses that are considered to be quite dull have been successful in driving interaction with humorous images or videos. With Tumblr you need to offer a variety of content to spark interaction and keep your followers interested and engaged.

Before you get started have a look at the popular tags and also at what your competitors are posting. When you look out for what is being liked and reblogged it is easy to see what's working and what's not and with all the incredible visuals on Tumblr it really isn't hard to get inspired. Here are some ideas for the type of content you should be creating or reblogging on Tumblr.

Relatable content

Relatable content is one of the most popular types of content and drives likes and reblogs and comments. Relatable content is anything that your target audience can relate to and identify with, it's when your audience sees a piece of content and immediately thinks, "Yes, I can relate to that and this is exactly the way I feel when this happens". It's incredibly powerful because this content is immediately communicating to your audience that you understand them and you feel their pain or joy and you can empathise with them. With relatable content you are communicating with them on quite a deep level which all helps to build relationships and trust. This is why Someecards is so successful, most of their content is relatable.

Emotive content

Creating content that is capable of generating emotion is going to go a long way in creating loyalty and a deeper connection with your audience. This type of content is most frequently reblogged on Tumblr. Once you know your audience and their typical wants and desires it can be easy to create this type of content. When your audience starts to idenitify emotionally with your content they will start to identify emotionally with your brand too. You can do this with all types of posts, images, GIFs videos, text and quotes.

Educational content

Posting informative content about your subject is invaluable, this will help you to stand out as a thought leader and expert in your field. If your content is valuable and useful then your followers are likely to keep coming back for more and are likely to share your content too. Remember your audience are looking to find and share valuable content with their audience too and will want to be associated with any compelling content you create.

Informative

This could be about letting your followers know about a something that is happening like a Webinar, a trade show or event in the area, or a special offer, or any information that will be of use or value to them.

Entertaining/amusing content

Humour is always a winner on Tumblr and one of the most popular tags, the #lol tag is usually at the top of the list on www.tumblr.com/explore. People just love sharing funny stuff. Even if you did not create it yourself but you think it is going to appeal to your target audience then share it. The aim here is to amuse and entertain your audience, humour is a winner all round and not only does humour break down barriers it is also more likely to be liked and reblogged.

Seasonal Content

Posting content relating to important holidays and annual celebrations is a really good way to stay connected with your audience and keep your content up to date and timely.

Inspiring and motivational content

The truth is everyone has a bad day sometimes and needs a little bit of motivation or cheering up. A motivational quote will help to lift your audience and can really help to connect with them. If you know what your audience wants, what they aspire to and what their frustrations are then it is likely that you will be able to motivate them by posting content which inspires them. These types of post are also very shareable especially if put together with a colourful and inspiring image like a cartoon or photo.

Employee and behind the scenes content

If you have news about your employees and the great things they are doing then post it. Maybe they have been involved in a fundraiser or they have won an employee of the month award. Giving your audience a behind the scenes view of your business helps to keeps your business and brand looking real, authentic and adds human interest.

Shared Content
Whilst it is great to post most of your own content, don't be afraid to share other peoples content as long as it is relevant. The more valuable content you share the more valuable you will become to your audience and the more likely they will keep coming back for more. Sharing content is also incredibly important in building relationships with your fans, they are going to be far more open to your brand if you are supporting theirs.

Statistics
People love statistics which relate to their niche and infographics do very well on Tumblr. Because most of us are visually wired, infographics can be one of the best ways to communicate information and numbers, they are easy to digest, fun to share and engaging. A picture really is worth a thousand words. To create infographics there are numerous sites online like www.piktochart.com and www.infogr.am

Questions
Asking questions about subjects that your audience may be interested in is a great way to encourage comments, interaction and community. People love to share their opinions and thoughts and love the opportunity to communicate, contribute and be heard. Even if you are posting an image or video it's really practice to ask a question.

Ask me a question post
Asking your followers to ask you a question is a great way to encourage interaction. You could also post a selection of questions and ask them to select one for you to answer.

Post about a book
Writing a post about a book you have read that may appeal to your target audience is a very effective way of delivering valuable content especially if it is going to help them in some way.

Top Ten lists

People love lists about who or what is top or best. Lists spark interest and this is most probably because people like to compare their choices and judgement with others. Some may like to see that their opinions match others and feel they are right in that choice or others may feel comforted by the fact their choices are not the same and they are unique.

Controversial

Posting a controversial statement can spark great conversation and interaction, remember people love to voice their opinions, have an input and be heard. It may be a good idea to stay out of the discussion here as you do not want to lose followers and you need to be sensitive to your audience in order not to upset them so be careful with what topics you pick.

Special offers

Tumblr is a great way to get the message out about the special offers you have running but you will need to be careful not to post them too often or they just appear like advertising and bad noise in your audience's news feed. You need to make sure that what you are offering is of real value, that it is exclusive to your followers and you are offering them a deadline to redeem the offer.

Contests and sweepstakes

Contests and sweepstakes are always a great way to gain popularity, grow your audience, build your brand and build your opt-in email list. With contests your audience can have great fun with your brand and they can also create high levels of engagement. Creating and running contests on Tumblr will be covered in more detail later on.

Voting polls & customer feedback

Creating a poll is a great way to encourage engagement on Tumblr. You can embed polls to Tumblr by using ww.polldaddy.com Polls can help give you a deeper understanding of your audience and also offers you valuable feedback about products or services.

Tips and tricks
Offering a weekly or daily 'Top Tip' can keep your audience hooked and returning again and again for the latest information and are a great way to increase loyalty and build relationships. Tips can be anything from instructions on how to do something to information about a useful app.

News and current events
Offering information about the latest news that relates to your niche is a certain way to keep people interested and sharing your content. Being current and up to date with local news is really useful to your audience and it keeps your business looking fresh and up to date. To keep up to date with news, subscribe to news feeds and blogs that offer news on your industry or your local area.

Negative content
People always like to hear about what not to do, for example: 10 Things not to do on a first date or 10 things not to say in a job interview, the list of possibilities for this type of post are endless and can create a great deal of amusement and interest.

Music if you are a musician
If you are a band and want to promote your music then there is no better way to promote your material than by posting links to your music and videos on Tumblr.

Fill in the blanks posts
Getting your audience involved with your content is a very powerful way of creating engagement. Fill in the blank posts can be way of creating engagement and conversation, for example:
- I love going to _____ on my holidays because…
- My monday morning must have this_____
- I always take _____ on holiday.

Caption this

Posting a photo and then asking your audience to caption it is a really effective and light hearted way to drive engagement and you could also turn this into a contest. You can use images from stock photo sites or sites like Flickr as long as you check the terms of use. When using images make sure you choose images which are either very interesting, humorous or inspiring.

Case studies

Case studies are a really effective way to demonstrate how something works with real examples. You can use case studies to show how your customers have used your products or services to benefit them in some way. You can also use them to demonstrate a principle or method of doing something by using other businesses as examples.

Internet Memes

Meme comes from the greek word 'mimema' which means something imitated. An internet meme is a style, action or idea which spreads virally across the internet. They can take the form of images, videos or hashtags. There are plenty of tools and apps out there to help you create memes such as www.memegen.com and imgur.com which are popular ones.

Like versus share votes

This involves combining two competing images in one post and then asking your audience to vote for which image they choose by liking or sharing. This is a really quick way to expand your reach and get your brand out there. To be successful at this you really need to have good subject and one that most people identify with.

Your blog

Creating regular blog posts is a very effective way of getting your followers onto your website. Make sure you always include an image to provoke interest and asking a question can create intrigue and curiosity.

Greetings
Simply posting an attractive image or a wishing your followers good morning, good night or to enjoy their weekend will go a long way in breaking the ice and building relationships. These types of posts help to make positive associations with your brand.

Testimonials
You may have received a review on Google Places or Foursquare or simply a message from someone. Posting about good things that people write or say about you contributes to your social proof and builds trust. Remember people will believe more in what others say about your business than what you, as the owner, say about it.

Behind the scenes
Behind the scenes photos may seem uninteresting to you but to others they can bring your business to life and show an authenticity to your brand. You can show how a product is made or just show a glimpse of yourWednesday employees at work.

GPOYW This stands for Gratuitis picture of yourself Wednesday. This has been a tradition on Tumblr since about 2008 and is a fun way to show a photo of yourself from time to time.

Top Tips for Posting Content on Tumblr
Create a content calendar
Creating a content calendar will help you not only stay on topic but will also help you to pace yourself. If you do not have one then you may find you are frequently posting at the beginning and then suddenly run out of ideas later on. Once you start mapping your ideas out you will be able to work out just how frequently you will be able to post. There are many calendars online that can help you with this task including Google Calendar which offers you the opportunity to colour code your entries.

Mix it up

Tumblr gives you so much opportunity to keep your feed interesting and varied. Offering a variety of content will keep your audience interested and wondering what your next post will be.

Tag your posts

Tags are big on Tumblr and if you want to get found then you need to tag your posts. Tagging is important because people not only search for tags they also follow tags. To add tags simply create your post and then add the keywords relevant to your blog post in the tag space below your post. When you start typing in the tag field you will find Tumblr will offer you various words relating to your letters you are typing in which you can choose as if you wish. Make sure you only tag your post with the relevant tags and try to be as specific as possible. On the right of your dashboard you will see that you can actually track tags.

Reblog

When you reblog content it not only appears on your Tumblr but also in the dashboard of your followers. Reblogging is a great way to offer great content to your audience without having to create it all yourself and if you choose wisely you can associate yourself with some great blogs and great content which will help towards building your brand. When you do reblog it's a really good idea to add your own comment and let your followers know why you have reblogged and why that particular piece of content may be relevant to them.

Post frequently

Tumblr is quite fast moving and as long as you have content that is relevant and interesting and not too much of the same you can really post as much as you like. To make sure you show up in the feed of people you are following you need to post content frequently.

Use the Queue
If you want to publish a string of posts while you are offline you can do so with the queue. The queue lets you stagger posts over time and you can queue between one and fifty posts a day. When you go to publish your post simply click the down arrow next to where it says 'Post' and then click on 'Add to Queue.'

Optimise your posts for search engine optimisation
Make sure you add keywords to your title and if you are posting an image add important keywords to your description in the space for your caption. When you are adding a link to a post make sure you add a description of the content of the post and the content of the link you are pointing it to.

Add anchor text
Tumblr allows you to add anchor text to your links. You can direct your audience to your website with a link and create anchor text with popular keywords from your industry which also helps with search engine optimisation.

Schedule your posts
Tumblr allows you to schedule your posts for particular dates and times in the future. This is really handy for keeping your account active while you are away from the office. Simply click on the down arrow when you go to post your update and click on 'schedule'. You can either enter the date like this 'Next Tuesday, 4pm' or 'mm/dd/yy 12:34am' then click 'Schedule'.

The personal touch
As with all social media it's about being social, being unique and authentic. To help your audience identify with you and become friends with your brand you need to add your personality. You can do this by adding a personal touch to your comments by explaining why you are posting, what you are posting and how it will help your audience in some

way.

Watermark your posts

There are two schools of thought on this subject but it is often a good idea for marketing to watermark your images or brand them in some way. Often images will get copied and if people want to find the original source of an image a discreet watermark with your web address or Tumblr URL can help. Watermarks are not going to protect your images totally but they will help you get found and make people think twice before they decide to copy them.

CHAPTER FIVE

BUILDING YOUR AUDIENCE ON TUMBLR

THE MORE FOLLOWERS you gain on Tumblr the more chance you have of your posts being reblogged. Unlike other social networks the number of followers is not published, but what is visible is the number of notes on your posts. This makes Tumblr refreshingly different from other networks because your credibility is no longer based on your follower count. Even though building up a sizeable following is important, you can really devote your time to finding the right audience and creating high quality content without having to worry about how your follower count looks. Statistics show that the majority of reblogs on Tumblr are from followers of your followers so the more followers you have the more opportunity you have of increasing your reach.

Here are some tips and strategies on how to build a targeted audience on Tumblr:

Post quality content
The best way to build your audience is to create quality content. When you post quality content you are likely to get reblogged and shared on other platforms too. A post that is reblogged will be seen by your followers followers and so it is very powerful and you can reach out to a wide area on Tumblr.

Find Friends
Tumblr offers you the opportunity to find your friends via Facebook and your email. Simply click on 'Find blogs' from your dashboard or go straight to www.tumblr.com/lookup

Follow other users
When you follow other Tumblrs it brings attention to your Tumblr. It's really important to follow back anyone who follows you and really helps to build relationships on Tumblr. On Tumblr your follower count is not displayed so nobody knows how many people you are following, or how many people are following you!

Be the face of your blog
Tumblrs with faces are more likely to get followed than those without so it is a good idea if you are a personal brand to have a picture of yourself on your Tumblr so you can make that personal connection with your followers.

Use hashtags to find your target audience
By searching for hashtags about the subjects you think are important to your target audience you will be able to find them.

Use tags in your posts
You want to make sure you appear in as many Tumblr searches as possible. Tumblr search relies on tags so you need to make sure that all your posts are tagged properly with the relevant tags that relate to your content and are in line with your target audience's interest. Adding between 7 and 11 tags is probably the right number without over using tags

Reblog, like and comment
Liking, reblogging and commenting (if users have this function installed) is a great way to build relationships. Reblogging is incredibly powerful on Tumblr and whether you reblog from the original source or not, the action of reblogging will appear on the original tumblr account, the post will also display all the people who reblogged which will offer you even more exposure. There is an art to reblogging. Any text or images that are added to the reblog will be seen by your followers and by your followers

followers if they reblog. It is therefore a good idea to personalise your reblog by adding an interesting comment and by telling your followers why you have reblogged this, however make sure you don't remove any of the content that was posted by the original source.

Send fan mail

Fan mail is just that and should only be used to compliment someone on their blog or on a particular post. You can send unlimited fan mail, up to 500 per day to the blogs you follow but you will have to wait at least 48 hours after following them before you can send a mail. Fan mail is a great way of drawing attention to your blog and can be accessed at the top of your dashboard.

And now @mention

Tumblr has recently introduced the @mention. So now if you want to get somebody's attention in a post you can now @mention their username.

Encourage interaction

The more interaction you allow the better, so make sure you allow replies from the people you follow and the users who are following you and let people ask you questions. You can turn on all these features in your settings.

Add Tumblr buttons

You can add your Tumblr buttons to your website or blog here http://www.tumblr.com/buttons

Announce your presence

Announcing your presence on other networks like Facebook, Twitter and Google + is a great way to build your following. The more people that share your content on Tumblr the more you will widen your reach. You can choose to automatically share your posts with Facebook and Twitter or you can selectively post the updates you want to promote on those platforms. If you are going to be posting frequently on Tumblr then it's probably not such a good idea to link your Tumblr to Facebook, as fans on Facebook are less tolerant of frequent posting.

Allow submissions
Allowing others to submit posts to your Tumblr is a great way to get others to contribute and provide content while at the same time building relationships. You can enable this feature in your settings, simply click the gear icon and 'Let people submit posts'. Nothing will get posted to your blog without your approval.

Add the Facebook like button and Twitter buttons to your Tumblr and your posts
You can add your Facebook like button to your Tumblr. Simply visit this page https://developers.facebook.com/docs/plugins/like-button/ and get the code by entering your Tumblr URL where it says 'URL to like.' When you have the code, click ' Customize' then 'Edit HTML' and pick the place where you want to add the code, add and then click 'Update Preview' and save.

To add a like button to your post you can simply add this code next to your post. Again you need to visit 'Customize' and 'Edit HTML' and then place it where you want to in the body. The best place is just before where it says "{/block:Posts}"
<div><iframe src="http://www.facebook.com/plugins/like.php?href={Permalink}&layout=standard&show-faces=true&width=450&action=like&colorscheme=light" scrolling="no" frameborder="0" allowTransparency="true" style="border:none; overflow:hidden; width:300px; height:75px"></iframe></div>

To do the same with Twitter simply visit this page, https://about.twitter.com/resources/buttons

To add more sharing buttons go to www.sharethis.com and get the code and add it in the same way. Once you had added it will appear under each of your blog posts.

Tumblr train
www.tumbletrain is an imaginery train where the passengers are actually Tumblr users and are looking for followers. You simply get on the train (sign up) and then get exposed to the other passengers who will hopefully start following you. It definitely cannot harm joining the train but at the same time you cannot expect to get the most targeted followers however if these followers are going to share your content and widen your reach then it has got to be good thing. There are similar schemes available like www.tumblrfollowers.com. Joining as many as possible is good idea to kick start your following and getting the ball rolling with your content being shared.

Follow for follow
If you add this phrase into Tumblr search you will come up with all the users who want to be followed and will hopefully follow you back in return. You do not have to follow them all and it is probably advisable to be selective.

Get featured in Tumblr Spotlight
When you click on 'Find blogs' on the right hand side of your dashboard you will be taken to a page where you can search by category and also see blogs which have already been included in Spotlight. These blogs have been singled out for their original and unique creative content.

If you want to get featured in Spotlight and you feel your blog has enough content to show off your creativity then simply send a note to editors@tumblr including your URL and the category you would like to be featured in.

Guest blogging
Guest blogging on other people blogs is a good way to get some attention while you are building your audience. Find other blogs with similar topics and offer complimentary products and be on the look out for Tumblrs that allow you to post your content.

CREATING A CONTEST ON TUMBLR

Contests are always a great way to increase your reach and help increase your following on Tumblr. With Tumblr's flexibility and functionality it allows you to create great contests easily. Before going ahead you need to work out what it is you want to achieve from running a contest, is it to increase your following, build your opt-in or to promote a particular product? Once you have decided on this, here are the steps you need to take to set up a contest on Tumblr.

Check out Tumblr terms and conditions
Make sure you familiarise yourself with Tumblr's guidelines at http://www.tumblr.com/policy/en/contest_guidelines , for example, you are only allowed to offer prizes of up to $1000 without their permission and you are also not allowed to ask users to follow, reblog or like as a prerequisite for entering. The other thing you need to check are the rules for sweepstakes and contests in your particular country or state.

Pick your prize carefully
In order to gain the attention of your target audience it is really important to pick a prize that is relevant to your business and that your target audience will value. This way you can be sure that the majority of entrants will actually be interested in your product rather than offering a more generic type of prize that may get you a wider audience but will not necessarily be the right audience. Offering a gift card to purchase your products is a great way to appeal to the right audience and also a wider audience who will then have a choice of the products you are offering.

Decide on the type of contest

Are you going to run a simple sweepstake or ask your contestants to submit something like an image or video. Visual contests run very well on Tumblr and you can ask your entrants to submit their entries using the submit functionality which can be found in your settings. You can monitor all your entries and make sure the content is appropriate before displaying it on your Tumblr. If you are going to be asking your audience to submit artwork or images and then use them in some way you need to make sure you cover yourself legally and mention this in your terms and conditions.

Ask your contestants to tag their entry

This is particularly important if you are going to promote your contest on other platforms like Twitter and Instagram. When you pick your tag make sure it is unique and specific to your contest or business. This way you can search for your # hashtag.

Decide on the duration of the contest Decide on the duration of the competition. With photo and video competitions you will need to offer a longer time as entrants will require more time to take their photos or video. With sweepstakes the duration of the competition can be much shorter.

Set your rules and publish Tumblr allows you to create pages on your Tumblr so you can easily create a specific page for your contest outlining the rules and how to enter. Make sure you include details like who your contest is open to. Tumblr is global so you may not want to ship outside your country. Tumblr states that users under the age of 18 are not allowed to enter so make sure you include this rule. You also need to include the closing date for entries.

Create a landing page Tumblr gives you the functionality to easily add a page to your Tumblr so you can set up a page with images to promote your contest, add your rules and also ask them to submit their entry with their email address, contests are a great way to build your opt-in list. If you are promoting your contest on other networks you could also send them to an external webpage.

Create a compelling graphic You need to create an interesting graphic with an attention grabbing headline, for example; ' Enter to win a $50 Gift Card from 'your business name'.

Promoting your contest To promote you contest you will need to have built up a following already so you have followers to share your contest with. Even though you cannot ask them to share to enter they will most probably upload their own entry to their own dashboard and reblog it anyway. Make sure you add a banner to your website, you can also send out emails to your list announcing your contest and promote it on your other social networks as well.

Choosing the winner You will need to decide how you are going to choose the winner. Many contest organisers use random.org to generate a random number from the number of contestants. If you have a photo contest then you will need to decide how they are going to be judged.

Post Contest
Once you have picked or chosen your winners you can post your winners on your Tumblr and share your plans for any future contests. To keep your unsuccessful entrants happy it's a good idea to email them with a money off voucher or coupon and hopefully you will convert some into customers.

Advertising on Tumblr
Advertising on Tumblr comes in the way of sponsored posts for mobile, sponsored web posts, sponsored radar and sponsored spotlight. To advertise you need to contact the advertising team at Tumblr.

Chapter Six

Day to Day Activity

THERE ARE CERTAIN things that you will need to do on a day to day basis to run your campaign on Tumblr. It is a good idea to allot a specific amount of time and a particular time of the day to do this. Here are some of the things you will need to do:

Following your customer's Tumblr's

This is important if your customers are business owners themselves. Following their Tumblr or following your customers will go a long way in building relationships. By following you are showing them that you are interested in what they have to say and also helping them to achieve their goals by helping to build their audience.

Showing your audience you value and respect them

If you value and respect your audience they will most probably love, respect and value your business. Be kind, generous, offer as much help and value as possible, reply to their comments and make it obvious that you value them and are listening to them. Don't be afraid to be yourself rather than a stiff brand with no personality.

Everyone is aiming for likes, shares and comments so if you are helping others out by commenting and liking their content it is going to draw attention to your brand and they are more likely to take interest in your content. This is one area where the reciprocation rule works very well on Tumblr. Engaging with content will also draw attention to you and your brand and you will find that people will click on your name to find out who you are and they may very well follow you. Be friendly to your audience, be chatty, authentic, genuine and embrace the conversation. All this will all go a long well in building a positive image for your brand and will set you apart from your others who are continually ambushing their audience with self promotion.

Following influencers in your niche

Building relationships with key influencers in your niche is invaluable. Not only can you learn from their content but also these people can have literally thousands of followers, imagine if they follow you back and then share your content!

Dealing with negative comments

Every business at some time will have to deal with negativity from followers. Hopefully if you have a good product then this is not going to happen too often. There are ' trolls' out there who have nothing better to do than post negative comments, the best thing to do with them is just ignore them, delete their comments and block them.

However there will be real customers who have real concerns and complaints and may post negative comments publicly, there may also be people who really want to lash out to gain your attention as quickly as possible and spread the news to their friends too!

You need to deal with complaints as quickly as possible and be as transparent and authentic as possible. The best thing to do is to apologise and say how sorry you are to hear of the inconvenience they have been caused and offer to continue the conversation and deal with their concern by either private message or telephone. You can then deal with this privately, give your customer the full attention they deserve and decide on your next course of action or compensation.

CHAPTER SEVEN

Measuring and Monitoring your Results

MEASURING AND MONITORING your results and performance against your original goals and objectives on a continual basis is essential. This is where many businesses go wrong, they carry on aimlessly posting content without checking to see what is working and what is not. Then after six months or a year they wonder why their campaign is making no positive difference at all.

When you measure your results you will discover so much information about your campaign which will allow you to steer your campaign in the right direction to achieve those SMART goals and objectives and stop anything that is not working.

When you originally work out your strategies and tactics for your campaign you will be estimating what you need to do to achieve your goals and objectives. However as you campaign runs you will see exactly what you need to do to achieve what you originally set out to do. For example, you may need to increase the number of people you follow to attract new followers or you may need to change the types of posts you make to increase engagement and reach. You
may need to increase your number of posts in order to get more likes or reblogs. Perhaps you need to increase the number of competitions you run to increase the number of opt-in subscribers. This is what it is all about, making your campaign work for you by constantly measuring your success against the goals set and then adjusting those objectives accordingly in order to achieve the results.

There are many tools to available to help you measure your campaign on Tumblr including Google Analytics and other third party sites.

GOOGLE ANALYTICS

Google Analytics can provide a huge amount of information to measure the effectiveness of your campaign including the following:

How many visitors are visiting your Tumblr.
How often are they visiting your Tumblr.
Which are you most popular posts.
Which search terms your visitors found you through. (This is incredibly important for future tagging.)
Where your visitors are coming from.

Adding Google Analytics to your Tumblr

The first thing you need to do is install Google Analytics to your Tumblr and also make sure you have set up Google Analytics for any other websites or blogs so you can see how much traffic Tumblr is creating for your other sites.

Some themes are already set up to let you add your Analytics code straight into the appearance box. Simply select your particular blog and then click on 'Customise' and then scroll down to see if there is a field where you can add your Google Analytics code and add the code.

If your theme does not support that here is what to do in Google Analytics and Tumblr:

Google Analytics
- Simply login or create a new Google account if you do not already have one
- Once you are in, click on 'Admin' and then click on 'Create new account' and add your account name, for example Tumblr my blog

- Then choose 'http://' in the drop down menu and add either your Tumblr URL or your custom domain.
- Then select your business category, country, time zone, read and accept the terms and conditions and then click on ' Get tracking code'
- Copy your tracking code and 'Save'

In Tumblr
- On your Tumblr dashboard select the blog you want to update and then click on 'Customize'
- You can either paste your Google Analytics tracking code into the description section or click on 'Edit HTML' and paste before "</head>"

To view your Tumblr metrics simply login to Google Analytics and select your blog

Google Analytics provides advanced reports that will let you track the effectiveness of your campaign and see how much traffic Tumblr is sending to your website or other blogs you may have.

The Overview Report This report lets you see at a glance how much conversion value is generated from social channels. It compares all conversions with those resulting from social.

The Conversions Report The conversions report helps you to quantify the value of social and shows conversion rates and the monetary value of conversions that occurred due to referrals from Tumblr and any of the other social networks. Google Analytics can link visits from Tumblr with the goals you have chosen and your E - commerce transactions. To do this you will need to configure your goals in Google Analytics which is found under 'Admin' and then 'Goals'. Goals in Google Analytics let you measure how often visitors take or complete a specific action and you can either create goals from the templates offered or create your own custom goals.

The Conversions report can be found in the Standard Reporting tab under Traffic Sources > Social > Conversions.

The Networks Referral Report The Networks Referral report tells you how many visitors the social networks have referred to your website and shows you how many pageviews, visits, the duration of the visits and the average number of pages viewed per visit. From this information you can determine which network referred the highest quality of traffic.

Data Hub Activity Report The Data Hub activity report shows how people are engaging with your site on the social networks . You can see the most recent URLSs that were shared, how they were shared and what was said.

The Social Visitors Flow Report This report shows you the initial paths that your visitors took from social sites through your site and where they exited.

The Landing Pages Report This report shows you engagement metrics for each URL. These include page views, average visit duration and pageviews and pages viewed per visit.

The Trackbacks Report The Trackback report shows you which sites are linking to your content and how many visits those sites are sending to you. This can help you to work out which sort of content is the most successful so you can create similar and also helps you to build relationships with those who are constantly linking to your content.

Tracking Custom Campaigns with Google Analytics

Google Analytics lets you create URL's for custom campaigns for website tracking. This helps you to identify which content is the most effective in driving visitors to your website and landing pages. For instance you may want to see which particular posts on Tumblr are sending you the most traffic, or you may want to see which links in an email or particular banners on your website are sending you the most traffic. Custom Campaigns let you measure this and see what is and what is not working by letting you add parameters to the end of your URL. You can either add you own or use the URL Builder.

To do this simply type 'URL builder" into Google and click on the first result. The 'URL builder form will only appear if you are signed into Google. You then need to add the URL, that you want to track, to the form provided and then complete the fields and click 'Submit.' You will then need to shorten the URL with bit.ly or goo.gl/ . Once you have set these up you can track the results within Google Analytics.

THIRD PARTY TOOLS FOR MEASURING

Union Metrics

Unionmetrics is the official analytical platform for Tumblr. Union Metrics focuses on delivering simple social metrics that enable marketers and agencies to measure and improve their social media campaigns.

They offer a free service and a mini service for bloggers and plans for brands and agencies. All plans offer information on blog engagement, follower and content analysis and paid plans offer Google Analytics integration and plans for brands offer competitor blog tracking and keyword based topic analysis as well.

Numblr

Numblr offers a free analysis for key metrics for Tumblr blogs. You can track your note to post ratio , type of post breakdown and percentage of original content. Numblr also allows you to analyse any other Tumblr blog so it's great for checking out the competition.

Chapter Eight

Building your Brand with Tumblr

YOUR MAIN AIM through this whole process is going to be to connect, capture and convert your prospects through your website or blog, through Tumblr and through other social networks and this involves the following:

- **Connect** Your product needs to be the connection between your prospect and what they need, so the first thing you need to do is connect those two things. In order to do this you need to identify who they are and find them out of all the millions of people on the internet and then connect with them by offering them something they want or need.

- **Capture** Once you have found them you need to capture them on your website, blog, Tumblr or any other social media platforms. This is so you can continue your relationship with them either by email or through Tumblr and continue to communicate your brand message. To do this you need to offer them some sort of incentive so you can capture their name and email address.

- **Convert** When you have captured your prospect you need to convert them into a paying customer by nurturing them and continuing to build a relationship by offering them the content they want through email and Tumblr and then moving them toward signing up for a special or exclusive offer.

To achieve this successfully you are going to need to have a well defined brand and that brand needs to be communicated through everything you do or say through Tumblr, through your website, blog and your email campaign.

Whether you are a one person small business, large corporation or an organisation, your brand is one of the most important attributes of your business. Your brand is what you want your prospects and customers to respect, trust and fall in love with so they will buy and continue to buy your products and services. Your brand is what is going to set you apart from any other business and what will give your business the competitive edge.

Never has there been a better time for your business to build your brand and communicate your brand message to your target audience than through Tumblr. Your brand is the main ingredient for success and Tumblr is giving you the channel to communicate it. You can communicate with your audience everyday and if you get it right and connect the right brand experience with the right target audience you are onto an all round winner.

It may be that you have a well established brand already, maybe you have not created your brand yet or it just needs some tweaking or fine tuning. Maybe you are not exactly sure what your brand is, or maybe you feel it needs a complete overhaul. Whatever your situation is, you need to know that your brand is going to underpin your whole Tumblr campaign and it needs to be strong, clear, well defined and consistent. Once you have defined your brand your business is going to create it, be it, communicate it, display it, picture it, speak it, promote it and most of all be true to it. This chapter is going to take you through everything you need to know and do to define and create your brand so you can get into the hearts and minds of your target audience by communicating the right message and brand experience.

There are many definitions of the word brand but this is the one I like best because it incorporates pretty much all the necessary information you will need to help you to define your own brand.

Brand, the definition
Your brand is more than a name, symbol or logo, it is your commitment and your promise to your customer. Your brand is the defined personality of either yourself as an individual brand or your product, service, company or organisation, it's what sets you apart and differentiates your business from your competition and any other business. Your brand is created and influenced by your vision and everything you stand for including; people, visuals, culture, style, perception, words, messages, PR, opinions, news media, and especially, social media.

Why is your brand so important to your business?
Branding is important because it helps you and your business build and create powerful and lasting relationships by communicating everything you want to say about your product or service to your prospects and customers. A strong brand encourages loyalty and will ultimately create a strong customer base and increase your sales by doing the following:

- Demonstrating to your prospects and customers that you are professional and committed to offering them what you promise
- Making your business easily recognisable
- Creating a clear distinction from your competition
- Making your business memorable
- Creating an emotional attachment with your audience
- Helping to create trust
- Helping to build customer loyalty and repeat custom
- Creating a valuable asset which will be financially beneficial if you sell your business
- Creating a competitive advantage

To do all the above you are going to have to find a way to get into the hearts and minds of your customers so they will ultimately buy and continue to buy your products or services. Before launching your campaign and setting up profiles, posting content and engaging, you will need to have a clear picture of exactly what your brand is, or what you want your brand to be. You will need to define exactly how your brand is perceived now, how you want your brand to be perceived, where your business fits into the market, who your target audience is and how you want your business to develop in the future.

To do this you need a deep understanding of your business and the people who are going to be most interested in your products and how you are going to serve them. When it comes to defining your ideal target audience you need to work out which of your products are the most popular and which are the most profitable so you can focus your efforts in finding and connecting with the right audience and then creating the right brand experience for them.

Your Vision/Your Story

If you want to create a strong brand then when of the first things you need to do is create a clear visual picture of how you see your business now and in the future. This is about daring to see what your business could be without constraints or limitations.

This exercise will not only help you to work out what you want to achieve financially and creatively but also makes you focus on what really matters and will help you to create your own unique voice and story. This is incredibly important when it comes to your branding as this is what is going to make your business stand out from others and give you that edge.

To do this you need to get away from all distractions and think about how you would like to see your business grow and develop in the next three years. This is more than just putting a mission statement together, this is about your core business beliefs, why you are doing it, what you want your business to be and how you want to be perceived in your market. To help you do this you will need to ask yourself the following questions and record your answers:

- Why did you originally start your business or why are you starting a business?
- How did your original business idea come about?
- What changes are you looking to make in peoples lives?
- What are you hoping to achieve?
- What aspects of your business are really important to you?
- What are your hopes and dreams?
- What is your definition of success?
- What sort of turnover and income defines that success?
- How many employees does your business have?
- Why are you in business?
- What are your core values in your business?
- What impact do you want to have?
- What influence do you want to have?
- What sort of things do you want the media to be saying about you?
- What do you want your customers to be saying about you ?
- How you want to be portrayed on social media?
- How many Tumblr followers do you want ?
- What markets are you in? Are you local, national or international?

Once you have completed this exercise you will have all the material you need so that you can create the unique experience required to make your business stand out from all the others in your niche. This is the first step towards creating a brand for your business, this is the beginning of your story.

Defining your Brand

Whether you are responsible for defining and creating and developing your brand in-house, or you are employing a local branding and marketing agency, you will need to carry out an analysis of your business to define your brand. Completing the following exercise will help you to define and find clarity about your brand:

- A factual description of what your business is and the purpose of your business.

- Describe your product or service in one sentence ?

- List all your products and/or services.

- What are the benefits and features of all of your products?

- Which are your most profitable products/services?

- Which are your most popular products/services?

- Who are your ideal customers for each of your products or services? (Consumer or business, age, gender, income, occupation, education, stage in family life cycle.)

- Out of these customers who are the ones who are most likely to buy your most profitable products?

- Is the market and demand large enough to provide you with the number of customers you need to buy your most profitable products and achieve your financial goals?

- If your answer to the previous question is no then ask yourself the same question for each of your other products.

- Who are your three main competitors? (Have a look at their Tumblr account.)

- What distinguishes your business from your competition? What special thing are you bringing to the market that is of real value? What is your unique selling point? What solutions are your products offering your customers that will meet their needs or solve their problems?

- If you are already in business then write down what your customers are already saying about your business. What do think they would say about how your product or service makes them feel emotionally (you may need to ask your customers if you do not already know). What qualities and words would you use to describe the personality of your business as it is now. Here are some examples of words you may wish to use: high cost, low cost, high quality, value for money, expensive, cheap, excellent customer service, friendly, professional, happy, serious, innovative, eccentric, quiet, loud, beautiful, relaxing, motivating, sincere, adventurous, amusing, charming, decisive, kind, imaginative, proactive, intuitive, loving, trustworthy, extrovert, vibrant, transparent, intelligent, creative, dynamic, resourceful.

- Now whether you are already in business or starting out write down all the words to describe how you want and need your brand to be perceived and what qualities you want to be associated with your brand in order to match the needs and expectations of your ideal customers. If you are already in business hopefully this will be exactly the same from how you perceive you are at the current time.

- What is the evidence that backs up what you have said about your brand, this could be customer testimonials or any evidence about product or service quality.

- What is the biggest opportunity for your business right now?

- What products are you thinking of introducing in the near future?

How to get into the Hearts and Minds of your Target Audience

Your target audience is your most important commodity as they are your future customers and ambassadors of your business. Every single one of them is valuable and every single one of them can make a difference to your business. This can be because they are actually going to buy your products or simply spread the word by interacting with you on Tumblr.

However it's a big social world out there, the possibilities of finding new people are limitless but targeting everyone is not the solution. The biggest mistake you can make is trying to reach everyone and then not appealing to anyone. Your first step is to identify exactly who the people are who are going to be interested in your products or services and then you need to find out everything about them. You need to get inside their heads and work out what motivates these people, what they are interested in, what their needs, hopes, aspirations and fears are and what are their dreams. Your product or service is the link between them and what they want. When you know this you can tailor every single message or piece of content towards them.

When you know exactly who your ideal customers are, Tumblr offers you the opportunity to go and find and reach them. It's then up to you to capture them so you can continue to communicate with them. When you know everything about your customers you are more likely to speak the right language to be able to communicate with them and build trust to the point where the next natural progression is for them to buy your product.

It's only when you truly understand your audience you can start converting them into customers. Once you know you are targeting the right audience, you can confidently focus every ounce of your effort creating exactly the right content, nurturing them, engaging with them and looking after them. It's only a matter of time before they will buy your product.

Creating your ideal customer persona or avatar

The following exercise is absolutely essential and your answers to the questions will be the very information that is going to help you communicate with your customer in the right way, by providing them with the right content and the correct brand experience. Once you have done this exercise you are going to own some very powerful information. If you do not do this exercise it is very unlikely that you are going to be able to truly connect with your target audience in the way that is necessary to build trust so that you can ultimately convert them into your customers.

Your answers to the questions in the previous section will have given you a clear idea of which types of customers you need to target to give you the best chance of achieving your financial goals. You now need to find out everything about them so you can get your brand into their hearts and minds. The best way to do this is to create an imaginary persona or avatar of your ideal customer and you can build this picture by finding out the following:

- Describe your ideal customer and include the following details, are they a consumer or in business, their age, gender, income, occupation, education, stage in family life cycle.
- Where do they live?
- What do they want most of all?
- What are their core values ?
- What is their preferred lifestyle?
- What do they do on a day to day basis?
- What are their hopes and aspirations?
- What important truth matters to them ?

- What motivates and inspires them?
- What sort of routines do they have?
- What are their day to day priorities?
- How do they have fun?
- What do they do in their spare time?
- What subjects are they interested in?
- Which books do they read?
- Which TV programmes do they watch?
- What magazines do they read?
- Who do they follow on social media?
- Who are their role models?
- What really makes them tick?
- What are their fears and frustrations?
- What are their suspicions?
- What are their insecurities?
- What are their typical worries?
- What is the perfect solution to their worries?
- What are their dreams?
- What do they need to make them feel happy and fulfilled?

Big Questions

To answer the following questions you will need to step inside your ideal customers mind and imagine you are them.

- How do you feel when you find your product or service? What is your initial emotional reaction?
- What are the words that go through your head?
- How can I justify buying this product for myself?
- Are you ready to buy immediately?
- Do you have any suspicions that the product may not be what it says?
- What are those suspicions? And why do you have them?
- Do you need more convincing?
- What do you need to convince you that the product is right for

you?
- What do you feel when you have the product in your hand?

The reason why these are such big questions is because your answers to them will establish whether or not you have correctly defined your ideal customer and whether you have really understood their needs, desires and fears. If you are imagining yourself as your ideal customer and you are saying woohoo, ecstatically jumping up and down with glee, immediately buying the product or relieved that you have at long last found the solution to your problem, then you have created the right avatar. If not then you need to think again.

It's only when you have imagined yourself in the hearts and minds of your target audience that you are going to be able to connect with them on any emotional level. With the information from the above exercise you will have everything you need to produce exactly the right content to match the needs, desires and expectations of your ideal customer so that you can create the right brand experience and sell your products. This information is like gold.

COMMUNICATING YOUR BRAND

Once you are clear about what your brand is, who your target audience is and where you want your business to go, you will be ready to translate all this into your brand. Your brand needs to be consistent and extend to every aspect of your business, everything you do, everything you produce to promote your business and everything you say. It will also need to be evident throughout your social media campaign.

When you are clear about what your brand is, what it stands for and how you are going to stand out from other similar businesses you then need to work out how you can communicate this message in the best possible way. Your main aim here is to create an emotional connection with your target audience that is going to help them grow to love your brand, remember your brand and remain loyal to it. To do this you need to communicate your brand story through every aspect of your business including your social media campaign.

With the information you now have you are armed with everything you need to create a consistent brand and if you have not already done so you can either hand all this information over to a marketing agency or use it yourself to create all the following:

- **Your Logo** Your logo will give a clear guideline for all your promotional material including your website or blog, stationery, templates or any marketing material that needs to be created for online or offline promotion.

- **Your brand message** The main message you want to communicate about your brand.

- **Your tagline** A short, memorable statement about your brand that captures the personality of your brand and communicates how you or your product will benefit your customer.

- **All your 'about' descriptions** You can communicate your brand story through all your 'about' sections on all your social media platforms you are using.

- **The content you create for your business** Every piece of content you create for your business needs to be tailor-made for your target audience. You will need to pick who and what subjects or topics you want to be associated with your brand, as anything you pick to write about will be a representation of your brand.

- **Your website and/or blog** The about page of your website is probably the most visited page of any website and there is a reason for this, people want to find out about your business and they want to find out what is different or special about it. This is a great place to introduce and expand on the story of your brand, this is where you can really go to town and communicate your beliefs and how you are unique. Also the visual style of your website or blog and your unique voice should be evident throughout your site and be consistent with your brand.

- **Video content** Videos are an incredibly powerful way of creating a personal connection with your audience. Make sure you that whatever video content you produce and whatever you say is always consistent with your brand.

Chapter Nine

The Essential Tumblr Marketing Plan

BEFORE LAUNCHING INTO your campaign you will need to know exactly what you want your business to achieve and what you want to achieve through marketing your business on Tumblr. Without the necessary planning and preparation your campaign is very unlikely to succeed.

This next few chapters take you thorough everything you need to do to plan your campaign before actually posting content. In this chapter you will learn how to create your mission statement, set goals and objectives and plan the strategies and tactics you need to implement, to achieve those goals. In the following chapter you will learn exactly how to prepare your business, your website and blog and your email campaign so you can capture and convert.

Creating your Mission Statement

Many campaigns fail at the first hurdle simply because they do not have a clear idea about why they are undertaking a campaign or what they want to achieve. They set up a Tumblr and have little or no idea why exactly they are doing it, "Everyone else is doing it… we probably should too" Then they launch in without first articulating the purpose of their Tumblr campaign and aimlessly start posting content. Before long they realise that this is having no positive effect on their business and either give up or continue half heartedly.

Once you have defined your brand and your target audience you will need to produce your mission statement for your social media campaign. Your mission statement is vital for your business as a whole and for your prospects and customers and should clearly state your commitment and promise to them as well as communicating your brand message. You will be able to include this in your Tumblr description. To create your mission statement simply follow these for four easy steps:

- **Describe what your business does** Describe exactly what you do and what you offer and the purpose of your business.

- **Describe the way you operate** Include your core values, your level of customer service, your commitment to your customers. You can include how your core values contribute to the quality of your product or service

- **Who are you doing it for?** Who are your customers? Business owners, entrepreneurs, working women, gardeners, shop owners, etc.

- **The value you are bringing** What benefit are you offering your customers ? What value are you bringing them?

Once you have created your statement everyone will know exactly what you are about. You will know exactly what you need to deliver to your customers. Your employees will know what is expected of them. Your customers and prospects will know exactly what your promise is, and what they can expect when buying your products and services.

SETTING YOUR GOALS AND OBJECTIVES

Setting goals and objectives is the key to your success on Tumblr. Once they are set you will be ready to plan and create the strategies and tactics to achieve those goals and objectives and you will be able to review and measure the success of your campaign.

Definition of a goal

A goal is a statement rooted in your business's mission and it will define what you want to accomplish and offer a broad direction for your business to follow. The three main goals of any business will ultimately be to increase sales, to reduce costs and to improve customer service and each goal will have a direct effect on the others. Here are some examples of goals and objectives within those three main goals:

1. To increase revenue and generate sales

- To increase website traffic.
- To increase brand awareness through Tumblr.
- To build a reputation as an expert within the industry.
- To build a loyal and engaged community on Tumblr.
- To increase the number of customers from word of mouth and referrals.
- To increase the number of sales.
- To increase average spend per customer.
- To increase the number of leads generated.
- To introduce new products.
- To increase online visibility.
- To promote an event.
- To build a highly targeted list of email subscribers.
- To connect with new customers.
- To build trust and build relationships with prospects and customers.
- To put a content marketing strategy in place.
- To increase business in 'X' country/state.
- To become a thought leader in the your industry.
- To develop a new markets by introducing your products into 'X' country/state.
- To decrease spend on traditional forms of advertising and invest X amount in Tumblr marketing.
- To build relationships with key influencers on Tumblr.

2.) To reduce Costs
- To decrease spend on traditional forms of advertising and invest in Tumblr marketing.

3. To deliver customer satisfaction and retain customers
- To answer customer questions promptly.
- To respond to customer complaints promptly, politely and helpfully.
- To provide online help/technical support.
- To respond to customer feedback.
- To listen to your customers.

Setting measurable objectives

Once you set your broader goals then you need to get more specific and create SMART objectives (specific, measurable, attainable, relevant and time bound). Here is an explanation of exactly what each of those terms means:

- **Specific** You need to target particular areas for improvement.
- **Measurable** Your progress needs to be quantifiable and putting concrete figures on your goals is essential for success and is the only way to measure the effectiveness of your campaign.
- **Attainable / Realistic** You need to be realistic with the resources you have available and the results you are expecting need to be realistic.
- **Relevant** Your goals need to be relevant to the business climate you are in.
- **Time Bound** Make sure you set a realistic time period to achieve your goals. If a time is not set then things don't tend to get done.

Here are some examples of the sort of SMART objectives you should be setting:

- Increase sales of product X by X%

- To increase opt-in subscribers from Tumblr by X per week.
- To build an audience of X number followers on Tumblr within one year.
- To increase number of followers by X per week.
- To increase website traffic from Tumblr by X times.
- To increase opt-in list subscribers by X per week
- Increase conversions from Tumblr by X per week.
- To increase the number of leads generated from Tumblr by X per week.
- To increase the number of new customers by X per month.
- To increase the average spend per customer by X.
- Introduce X number of new products every 6 months.
- To increase sales from X country/state by X%
- To decrease spend on traditional forms of advertising by X and invest X amount in Tumblr marketing.
- Utilise Tumblr to increase YouTube views by X people per week.

Choosing your Strategies and Tactics

Once you have set your quantifiable goals and objectives you are going to have to work out how you are going to accomplish them using Tumblr. You will need to think about the strategies and tactics you are going to use and they need to be quantifiable as well. Here are some examples of the strategies you may want to implement:

- To create content on Tumblr X times per day.
- To spend X hours per week looking for and curating content to reblog on Tumblr
- To make X% of posts photo/posts.
- To create X number of blog posts per week/month and post them on Tumblr with images.
- To post X offers per month/6 months on Tumblr.
- To run X competitions/contests per year on Tumblr.
- To create X Gifs promoting videos on YouTube per month.
- To spend X minutes per day liking, commenting and reblogging.

- To follow X influencers on Tumblr per week.
-

Of course at the beginning you are going to need to make an educated guess at the number of times you are going to need to do one thing to achieve another. As your campaign runs you will need to adjust certain aspects to achieve what you set out to achieve. For example, you may need to spend more time following other Tumblrs in order to increase your reach on Tumblr or you may need to spend more on advertising to increase your number of followers or you may need to change the type of content you are posting to increase the amount of engagement.

The only way you can do this is by constantly monitoring and measuring your results against the original goals and objectives you set and adjusting your campaign accordingly.

Creating your Tumblr Posting Calendar

Now you have your strategies in place you will have a good idea of the amount and type of content you need to post to achieve those objectives. One of the most challenging tasks of your Tumblr campaign is going to be to consistently deliver a high standard of content to your followers on a daily basis. You are going to need to post between one to four times a day. This does not mean you need to create numerous blog articles each day but you are going to need to communicate in some way and find unique ways for your audience to interact with your brand and offer some kind of value on a regular basis. This may seem daunting to begin with but you will be surprised how one idea leads to another.

To help you map out your content for the next six months or the year ahead you need to create a Tumblr posting calendar which is your key to consistent posting. There are many online tools and apps that can help you with this. Google Calendar is a very good calendar to use and lets you colour code the different types of post. You can also use Hootsuite, the social media dashboard to plot out your calendar or use a spreadsheet in Excel. There are also other online applications like www.trello.com

which has easy to use drag and drop features and using mind mapping applications like 'Simplemind' can really help when brainstorming for content ideas.

To get started you will simply need to map out and schedule the days of the week for each week of the year and decide what types of post you are going to create for certain days. You will need to balance the type of content in order to create variety and interest for your audience. You then need to create topics or themes and then break the year down into weeks/months and make a schedule. You can then add all the things that you are planning within your business, like offers, contests, product launches, webinars and then add all the things going on outside your business like public holidays and special events. You then need to incorporate all that information into your daily action plan.

It may seem daunting to look at a blank calendar but you will be surprised how it comes together when you start breaking it down into months, weeks and days. A posting calendar will help you keep your campaign focused and on track and in line with your brand and your marketing goals and also keep it balanced in terms of the subject and type of media you use. A calendar will help you look ahead and help you to incorporate your marketing plan into your Tumblr campaign. It may be that you are launching a new product, or maybe certain products tie in with specific holidays, you may have certain industry events you need to attend or are perhaps creating your own. Maybe you are going to run a competition at a certain time of the year, whatever it is you are planning throughout the year you need to include it on your calendar.

The following example shows just how by creating a regular weekly schedule you can really simplify the process of creating your social media posting calendar:

Week 1
Monday

AM	Inspirational quote image to start the week.
PM	Post GiF promoting YouTube video.

Tuesday

AM	Post weekly blog article on Tumblr with image.
PM	Post chat post.

Wednesday

AM	Post a cartoon that relates to your niche.
PM	Fill in the blank post.

Thursday

AM	Post an engaging question .
PM	Post or share an Infographic.
Special	Post contest photo and entry details.

Friday

AM	Share a business tip.
PM	Post a weekend photo wishing all a happy weekend.
Special	Holiday Weekend Post.

Saturday

AM	Post a question that is not business related.

Sunday

AM	Share a funny video.
PM	Post a relaxing image for a Sunday.

This is just an example and you obviously need to tailor make this to your business with the content that is important to your particular target audience.

Chapter Ten

Preparing your Business for Success

WHETHER YOUR SITE is being found through organic search, an advertising campaign, Tumblr or any other social media platform, all your hard work is going to be wasted unless you have put a system in place to capture leads and convert them into customers. This system has to start from the moment your prospect either hits your website, your blog or your Tumblr page and your ultimate goal is to convert your browsers into buyers.

Firstly the unfortunate fact is that the majority of your website visitors are unlikely to buy from you on their first visit and if you do not have a website that grabs their attention within the first couple of seconds then they will move very quickly onto another site. Secondly even if your site does catch their eye, they are still likely to check out other sites and still may not return. To make any kind of impact at all your site needs to grab their attention and then capture their email address so you can continue your relationship with them through email. This chapter is going to take you through steps you will need to take, from getting your website or blog ready, to setting up and creating your email campaign.

Email is still one of the most powerful ways to convert prospects into customers and has a conversion rate three times higher than social media conversion rates. That is not to say that your Tumblr campaign is any less important, as this is where you are going to find and nurture your leads and transfer them to your opt-in by either capturing them on Tumblr or on your website or blog. This chapter is going to take you through steps you will need to take from getting your website or blog ready, to setting up and creating your email campaign.

PREPARING YOUR WEBSITE FOR SUCCESS

Whether you already have a website or blog or you are creating a new site from scratch you need to make sure it has the necessary features to grab the attention of your target audience and capture their email addresses. Capturing the email addresses of your target audience has to be one of your most important goals when creating your website. Once your prospects have voluntarily submitted their email address you have the opportunity to build a relationship, communicate your message and promote your products and services on an ongoing and regular basis. A well thought out and crafted email campaign can immediately establish trust and favour with your subscribers. Don't forget that it is you who owns your opt-in list and nobody can take it away from you and as long as you are providing your subscribers value with great content they are likely to want to keep hearing from you. Remember you cannot rely on social media to continue your relationship as these platforms are changing all the time, you need to build your email list.

Once you have completed the exercise in the branding section and have your ideal customer persona or avatar you will have a clear picture of what your target audience's pain point or problem is and how your product can help solve their problem or make their life better in some way. If you have a blog, and most businesses today need a blog, you will also have all the tools you need to create the right content to attract your target audience. Armed with this information you are half way ready to putting a system in place to sell, so your products sell themselves and your website is working like an extra sales person selling your products 24/7.

When your visitor arrives at your site you have only three seconds to grab their attention. You need to connect emotionally with them and let them know immediately that they have arrived at the right place by communicating exactly how you are going to help them and what it is you are offering them.

Once they are on your site you then need to win their interest and confidence so that they will voluntarily submit their email address. To do this you will need to create a lead magnet and offer your audience something which is incredibly valuable to them for free. There are numerous ways you can do this and which one you use will depend very much on what type of business you are and what your goals are. If you are a business offering technical solutions then you could offer them a free trial, if you are offering information then you could offer them a free report, a short video training series or an ebook. If you are selling some kind of product or service you could offer them a money off voucher, these work particularly well for restaurants and the service industry as a whole. Whatever you are offering, it needs to be really good to attract your audience and get them to volunteer their email.

Here are the features you need to have on your website or blog or any landing page with a special offer.

- **Keep your design simple** Your site needs to have a clean and simple design and you need to communicate your most important message clearly and concisely to your target audience. Your most important content with any call to action needs to be placed above the fold, where they will be easily seen and your call to action should have an easily seen button link rather than just a text link.

- **Make your site easy to navigate** Really this is so important, try to use the minimum number of pages you can and make your menu titles as easy to understand.

- **Clearly communicate your message** You want your visitors to subscribe to your opt-in so you need to place your compelling offer with an image and title of the offer somewhere where it is visible. The message and benefit of your offer needs to be descriptive and specific.

- **Add a clear call to action** In order for your visitors to sign up they will need to be told what to do. Make sure you have a direct call to action, for example, 'Download your free ebook now' or 'Sign up for your discount voucher now.' Your call to action needs to be clearly visible with an eye catching button link which is much more effective than a text link.

- **Add clear contact information** Make it easy for your prospects to contact you by placing your contact details where they will be easily seen. With the technology available you can even add chat features so that as soon as your prospect arrives on your site a chat form appears asking if you can be of any assistance. Obviously you need the resources to be able to man this but it is an incredibly powerful way of quickly building trust and showing how much you value your website visitors by being available to answer any of their questions.

- **Email capture form** Your email capture form needs to be as simple as possible, preferably just asking for their name and email. You need to state on the form that their email address is safe with you and will not be shared with anyone. Make sure your form is in a prominent position and consider using a pop-up form that appears after 20 seconds after your prospect has arrived on your site. Your email sign up form needs to go at the top, the side and the bottom of your webpage and also on your 'about page' which is often the most popular page on your site.

- **Privacy policy** You need a clear privacy policy on your website and to make it clear that you will not be spamming them or selling their information.

- **Thank you page** Once your visitor has completed the form you will have them as a lead, but before you let them go you can send them to a thank you page where you can offer them the opportunity to share your offer with their friends by including social sharing buttons.

- **Mobile Friendly** You need to make sure your offer is easily visible and easy to complete on mobile. This is incredibly important as more and more people are purchasing from their mobiles and there is nothing more annoying for the user if the site is hard to navigate from their mobile.

- Don't add external links to other sites Be careful not to fall into the trap of wanting to make your site more interesting by adding lots of content and links to other external sites as this will only detract from your main goals and you'll end up sending traffic away from your site.

Landing pages

Landing pages are incredibly effective if you want to promote specific offers for specific products to specific audiences. A landing page is a page that is designed to give information about an offer and then capture a lead with a form for your visitor to complete so that the visitor can download or claim that offer. Landing pages are highly effective in capturing leads because they are designed to be specific in their goal, which is to capture the contact information of your visitor.

The landing page should have a clear uncluttered design and not have any links or navigation menus that could take your visitor away from the landing page and it should contain the following:

- A headline. (The title of the offer)
- A description of the offer clearly detailing the benefits to your visitor

- A compelling image of the offer
- A clear call to action. This can be in the form of an image or text
- A form to capture contact information. (The fewer fields that are required to be completed the more leads you will receive)
- A clear privacy policy on your website that makes it clear that you will not be spamming them or selling their information
- A thank you page leading them to another offer or social sharing

You can either ask your web developer to create landing pages or there are numerous tools available on the internet where you can easily create one, for example: www.leadpages.net www.unbounce.com www.launcheffect.com and www.instapage.com

SETTING UP AND CREATING YOUR EMAIL CAMPAIGN

Once you have created your lead capture system on your website, blog, or separate landing page and have your subscribers permission to send them your email you are going to need a really good email campaign to convert those leads into sales.

Email is still one of the most effective forms of converting leads into sales and email is more powerful than ever. Not only is it cost effective but it also provides one of the most direct and personal lines of communication with your customer. Once they have subscribed they have invited you into their inbox on a regular basis and producing valuable content for your subscribers will develop trust and deepen your relationship with your subscribers. Your email will also work hand in hand with your Tumblr campaign. As you build your relationship with your followers on Tumblr, they are more likely to deem your emails valuable and open them.

The first thing you need to do is set yourself up with a good email marketing provider and there are many you can choose from: www.aweber.com www.constantcontact.com www.mailchimp.com to name a few. It's important to use a system where you have a confirmed opt-in, this is when the subscriber is sent an email to confirm their email address. This confirms that you are gaining consent and legally protects you, it also helps you to keep a clean list and it protects you from sending emails to incorrect addresses. You can then automate your emails with an auto responder and send out emails automatically to a specific timetable.

Your next task is to plan and create your email campaign. Here are a few tips for doing so:

- **Be clear about your goals** You need to be absolutely clear from day one what you want to achieve through email. Are you using it to introduce a new product at some time? Are you launching an event? Whatever you do make sure you know exactly what it is that you want to achieve.

- **Keep it simple and in line with your branding** Make sure your email design ties in with your branding. Most email providers offer templates which you can add your own branding to, or you can get a designer to create a particular design. Keep it really simple, sometimes if things are too fancy they become impersonal.

- **Send a regular newsletter** Plan to send a regular newsletter email at least once a month and once a week if you can. You can also plan to send one off information about offers which tie in with special holidays and occasions throughout the year, or competitions or events that you may be planning.

- **Plan your topics** You need to plan the topics you want to cover in each email and this should tie in nicely with the plan for your blog articles. You then need to deliver high quality content which is tailor-made to fit with your subscribers interests and it needs to be so good that they are looking forward to the next email from you. If you are sending emails about offers then you need to show them clearly how these offers are going to benefit their lives.

- **Attention grabbing titles** This is where you need to get really creative. Your main goal here is to get your subscriber to open your email and you need to create a headline that is going to make your subscriber curious and inquisitive and eager to open your mail. Questions work really well as titles and you will often see your open rates increase. This is because people find questions intriguing and they feel like you are directly addressing them. Try and avoid the words that will trigger spam filters, simply search Google for a list of these words to avoid.

- **Be authentic and true to your brand** Write your emails in a style that your audience will grow to recognise, like and identify with your brand. Write so your subscriber feels like you are just writing to them. You need to establish yourself as a likeable expert for your subscribers. Try and create a personal relationship with them by addressing them by name and giving them a warm friendly introduction. Offering them the opportunity to connect with you and answer any of their questions by simply replying to your mail is a great way to create a connection and trust.

- **Keep it simple** Make sure your emails are simply constructed and straight to the point so you keep your subscribers' interest and get them quickly to the place you want them to go, like your blog, or your offer.

- **Include social sharing buttons** Include all your social sharing icons and links in your mail.

- **Make them feel safe** Make sure your subscribers are clear that their email will not be shared and that they can unsubscribe anytime.

- **Analyse your open rates** Most email service providers include statistics in their packages so you can analyse open rates, bounce rates, click through rates, unsubscribers and social sharing statistics. These results give you the opportunity to find out what is and what is not working.

CHAPTER ELEVEN

THE ICING ON THE CAKE

FOLLOWING ALL THE steps, instructions and strategies is going to go a long way to making your campaign succeed, but what does it take to make you really good? If you have ever followed or are following certain brands on social media you will probably have discovered that there are certain brands or businesses that stand out from the crowd. These are the brands and businesses that seem bigger than their products. These are the ones who usually have a sizeable and highly targeted audience, the best quality content, the greatest amount of interaction and engagement and they often post viral content. They literally have their audience hanging on their every word and get the highest open rates for their emails. They appear to understand their audience and relate to them by going out of their way by either helping them to achieve their dreams, calm their fears or confirm their suspicions and offer them incredible value. It is obvious by the interaction that they have built a loving and respecting community and you can be almost sure that all this is transferring to their balance sheets. These businesses are what I call, 'The Social Media Superstars' they are the game changers and they truly know how to leverage the power of social media to work for their business.

These 'Social Media Superstars' can often be compared to those party animals, the ones who always seem to be the most popular at any party and are more often than not surrounded by an audience of engaged and happy people having a great time. These people also always seem to be the most interesting, the most interested, the most charismatic, the most engaged, and they almost always tend to be good listeners as well. So how can you emulate this scenario and what does it take to stand out from the crowd in Tumblr marketing?

It's all about your audience and a few other things!
The reasons these individuals, businesses and brands are good at social media marketing is not because they have particular powers, it's not by chance or by coincidence, it's because they know that it's all about the audience and a few other things!

Of course your aim is to ultimately benefit your business but in order to do this you need to make it all about your audience and what they want. If you give them what they want by either making their life better or easier in some way or solving a problem they may have, then you are going to build a valuable base of followers who trust you, open your emails and who are ready to go to the next step and buy your product. You will find that your followers will become ambassadors and advocates and will then be doing the work for you by sharing your content and promoting your brand in the most powerful way, word of mouth. To achieve this and stand out from the crowd you need to go the extra mile by doing the following:

- Being fully committed and positive about your campaign and in it for the long term
- Totally believing in what you are offering, This could be your product, your service or yourself if you are a personal brand
- Making it all about your audience, knowing exactly who they are, what makes them tick, what they need and how to connect with them
- Putting your audience's needs above your own and demonstrating the rich content and service you provide
- Putting the relationship with your audience first, by listening to them, understanding them and embracing conversation where you can
- Offering your audience incredible value with free information and advice

- Being authentic and true to your brand

So if there is one piece of insight I want to leave you with it is this:

IT'S ALL ABOUT YOUR AUDIENCE and WHAT THEY WANT
I really hope you have enjoyed the book, that you have found it of great value and you will continue using it as your manual for your success on Tumblr. The world of Social Media is continually changing and it is my commitment to keep updating the books as and when these changes happen. If you would like to continue receiving these social media updates by email please sign up at www.alexstearn.com

Lastly, I would love your feedback about the book and would be very grateful if you could take just a moment to leave a review on Amazon and of course please feel fee to contact me if you have any questions at alex@alexstearn.com

I have also written a series covering all the major social media platforms including: Facebook, Twitter, Google + , LinkedIn™, Pinterest, Instagram, YouTube and the big one, Make Social Media Work for your business. All are available on Amazon and Kindle. I will also be continually posting helpful and inspirational tips, building a community on Tumblr and look forward to connecting with you there or on any of your preferred social networks.

Website: www.alexstearn.com
www.alexstearn.tumblr.com
ww.google.com/+alexstearn
www.facebook.com/alexandrastearn
www.instagram.com/alexstearn
www.twitter.com/alexstearncom
www.pinterest.com/alexstearn
www.youtube.com/alexstearn
www.linkedin.com/in/alexstearn

Other Books in the Series

Make Social Media Work For Your Business

Make Facebook Work For Your Business

Make Twitter Work For Your Business

Make Instagram Work For Your Business

Make Pinterest Work For Your Business

Make Google + Work For Your Business

Make YouTube Work For Your Business